CONTEXTS

An Unauthorized Autobiography

Irving Zupnick

New Dialogue Press
Binghamton, New York
1999

Library of Congress Cataloging-in-Publication Data:

Irving Zupnick, *Contexts: An Unauthorized Autobiography*

1. Autobiography 2. Art

ISBN 1-883058-89-9

Published by *New Dialogue Press* and distributed by *Global Publications*
State University of New York at Binghamton
New York, USA 13902-6000
Phone: (607) 777-4495 or 6104; Fax: (607) 777-6132
E-mail: pmorewed@binghamton.edu

Table of Contents

Chapter I
MY LIFE AND TIME

A scholar's career, during which I published about 45 scholarly articles and a book, and read papers at various national and international conferences, on subjects ranging from ancient to modern art, and concerned with unconscious ideological content and hidden, or perhaps forgotten pictorial statements about once deeply-felt political or social issues, all of which I structured with inexorable rhetoric, has been an excellent preparation for writing other types of fiction, now happily liberated from the cumbersome scholarly apparatus, footnoting and photographic evidence, and certainly the excruciating agony of making, or is it remaking, history.

But let's face it, autobiography is even more relaxing than writing fiction. You don't even have to invent character and plot. And at my age, there is so much material that the big trick is to organize it into a meaningful structure, and to eliminate distracting extravagances.

Maybe in some lives "Time is of the Essence," (whatever that means) but not in my life.

According to my life, my experience tells me, time does not start in one place and then continue in a pointless unraveling. Instead, potential (pregnant?) events or even thoughts emit invisible beams that travel through some sort of medium in which I temporarily lose sight of them while they hide in ambush, waiting for an appropriate moment to pop out and reveal their underlying significance.

As I review my life on nights when I don't sleep too well, the events and impressions that I come across, seem to make more sense through cross-references or cross-filing than they did originally. Details of the past are not isolated. They seem to have a purpose that is activated when they find the right time to re-emerge and have an impact.

I don't know about you, but I am not planning to die. It would be totally irresponsible. It would mean that the world as I know it, would come to an end without me to remember it.

When I tell my kids and grandkids about my life, they seem to think that I am making it all up. Even total strangers look at me doubtfully. Only I know that all the strange and interrelated things that happened, and all the interesting and unusual people that I have met, are not figments of my imagination. (What is a "figment," anyway? According to *American Heritage Dictionary of the English Language*, it is "an arbitrary notion," or a "fabrication of the imagination." The word came to us through a Middle English mistranslation of the Latin word, *Fingere*, which meant, "to mold" or "to fashion"; and there is nothing arbitrary or unreal about it. What happened, happened. I did not have to figment any of it.

This has nothing to do with being afraid to die. As I said to my friend, Bob, and it seemed to cheer him up, although he knew that he was dying, "We all get dealt different hands in life, but it really doesn't matter, because in the end *The House Always Wins*."

Anyway, all of the dead people that I have seen in my life looked relieved, as if they had learned that it was no big deal. It is just that I would hate to see all of my amazing and interlocking experiences get dumped into some hole in the ground.

If I can leave some inkling of the world, as I know it, maybe some day someone will think, "This is incredible but I believe it."

Chapter II
...AND HE SPAKE

I remember that when I was quite young I could not fall asleep until I heard him come home from work.

I used to play in his World War I uniform until I outgrew it at the age of nine or ten. You see, he was only 5 foot 2 (according to his Discharge Papers) although he claimed to be two inches taller (maybe he grew while in the Army).

He used to tell me all kinds of stories. He told me that his dad, Abraham, had been a Colonel in the Army of the Russian Tsar; and that he quit and took his three children to America when he heard that the Tsar permitted or perhaps even sent the Cossacks to attack Jewish towns. My dad said that he watched as his dad threw a little box of medals over the side of their ship into the Ocean. I never met this Grandfather, who became a citizen in Louisville, Kentucky, of all places, and died before I was born.

My dad, Morris, and his brother, Lou, had an older sister, Sarah, who married a man named Zaffman, who peddled homemade cosmetics and then bought a general store in New Brunswick, New Jersey. She was unable to take the boys in, so Morris and Lou became street people, before it was a popular fashion, until they looked old enough to enlist in the Army, just before the U.S. entered the First World War.

They were both stationed in Fort Dix, N.J.; and the funny thing is that about 25 years later, when I was at Fort Dix myself, during the Second World War, I received a letter from a woman who wrote that she had been my dad's pen-pal, and that she had four daughters. I didn't want to get into that, so I wrote back that I hoped she would not be my son's pen-pal too; and I guess that she assumed that I was already married because of my rhetorical and as yet, unborn son, so that was the end of that.

Anyway, my little dad was a scrappy guy. His kid brother, at 5 foot 9, was even scrappier and he spent a good deal of time in the guardhouse for punching out guys who flirted with his girl friend, who worked in the Post Exchange. Lou later married her, but it didn't work out because she continued to flirt. Eventually he married a second time and lived above his grocery store in Philadelphia, and he had five wonderful daughters who are scattered around California, the last I have heard.

Now Morris, my dad, spent most of his adult life in uniform. After the Army, he was a streetcar conductor, and then, after getting the highest test score in the country, he became a letter carrier.

He used to enjoy telling me stories, which I never questioned. I was curious about The Big War, and in answer to my questions, he told me that he had been wounded in the Pedesfuss (he defined it as the bottom of the foot), and that he had received a medal for bravery from the French Marshall, Foch, who kissed him on both cheeks. I never asked to see the wound or the medal, but I told all of my friends, and he became something of a neighborhood celebrity; although apparently he had never left Fort Dix.

But one story he never told me, and I still wonder why.

I heard the story about a year after his death. My mother and I were invited to a party thrown by the Jewish War Veterans, and I met a man named Zimmerman, who was supporting himself on crutches, since he had lost his right leg all the way up to the hip.

When he saw my nametag he became very excited. "Was your father named Morris?" he asked. I nodded. "Was he at Fort Dix?" "Yes," I said. "Did he ever tell you how he got promoted to Corporal?" No, he didn't.

"Well," said Zimmerman, "We were in morning formation and he was on my right. The First Sergeant was a terrible anti-Semite, and he was going into a lot of the usual garbage, when out of the corner of my eye I saw your father lay his rifle down on the ground and leave. I could hear his boots going clump-clump on the ground as he moved around the Company, and then I saw him jump up on the platform and belt the Sergeant in his jaw. The Sergeant was a six-footer, but he went clean off the platform. His jaw was broken, and the Company Commander held a Summary court-martial a couple of hours later and I volunteered to be a witness. When the Captain heard the story, ---realize that the outfit was ten or fifteen percent Jewish,--- he busted the Sergeant to Private, promoted your father to Corporal and assigned him to the Orderly Room as Company Clerk."

Now, why didn't my dad tell me that story?

Anyway, when I was about ten years old and Head of the Simpson Street Gang, on the same block as the "Fort Apache the Bronx" Police Station, and probably about 5 foot eight, my dad looked up at me, laying down one of his rules of conduct, which was to be irrevocable inasmuch as he died not long after my thirteenth birthday, before I had the chance to become a revolting adolescent. He said, "Just because you are big, I don't *ever* want to hear that you are a bully. But on the other hand, if you have to defend yourself against someone bigger and stronger, or older than you, then you can use whatever is handy, a stick, a rock, or anything, to even things up. And if a grownup picks on you, you tell me, and I'll take care of it."

The first test of this obiter dictum came with "Tough Tony" Famigliari, who was Head of the Fox Street Gang on the next block.

I ran into him twice in the five years I lived in the neighborhood. The first time was when I was waiting to take a final examination in order to get promoted to 5A. I had been out of school for four months of the term (mumps, measles, chicken pox), but they said that if I could pass the final exam, I would be promoted.

I was in one of the school courtyards, waiting for the bell to ring, and I got bored. So I began to scale rocks to see if I could hit all three walls. As I scaled one rock, a kid came out of the door and the rock bounced off his head. He ran past me, screaming. A few minutes later "Tough Tony," who was about four years older than me, showed up. "Hey," he said, "You the guy who gave my kid brudder a hole in the head?"

A hole in the head! Wow! What did that look like? Could you see things through it? "Yeah," I said. "Come with me," says he.

So I followed him to Fox Street where his Grandma was sitting on the steps of their apartment house, leaning forward with her hands on her knees. "What do you bringa him for?" she said. "He'sa gotta no money for the doctor. Go back to school, boy." I went back, passed the exam, and was promoted.

The second time I ran into "Tough Tony," I was waiting in the back yard for the guys to come and play stick-ball. Meanwhile, I leaned the broomstick against the wall and practiced handball shots with my brand new Spaulding.

All of a sudden there was Tony on top of the wall. "Hey you," he said, "Gimme da ball." (A brand new, lively pink Spaulding I had just bought with my own money!) "Come and get it," I said.

The jerk started to climb down the wall, and I picked up the broomstick and smacked him with it, again and again, until it broke and I used the splintered end like a spear. He climbed back up the wall real fast, turned around at the top and wagged his finger at me. "You better not ever let me catch you alone," he threatened.

"Hey," I said, slashing the stick back and forth, "I'm alone now."

I don't remember ever seeing him again.

I only went to PS 20 for another year. In 5A, we got a brand new teacher, Miss Riley, and I fell deeply in love. She was a tiny person, with bright red hair and bright green eyes; and she loathed me. I had sinus trouble, for which I went through medical tortures I don't even want to think about (I would have sneered at the Spanish Inquisition); and I was always clearing my throat. The beautiful Miss Riley, being new on the job, was easily distracted by the noise I made.

She warned me. I said I couldn't help it. She began to lower my Conduct Grade until it was down to D-. Then she began to take my Classwork Grade down until it was a C.

But one day, the Principal came to our classroom and asked for me. He moved me into the 6A class, a whole year ahead. My Mom was very annoyed, even when her friend who worked in the Principal's Office, said it was because I had the highest IQ in New York, and they thought that my grades were dropping because I was bored. My Mom was annoyed because PS 20 only went up to 6B, and it meant that we would have to move pretty soon.

Incidentally, the Music Teacher, Miss Bryant, also had it in for me. I really enjoyed singing in the Auditorium, but no matter where I hid, she would hunt me down, put her finger to her lips and say, "Shhh ! You're a listener."

Anyway, when we moved, I went to PS 77, across from Monroe HS, and one of my best friends there was Jerry Gross. I was playing sandlot football with some high school kids, and Jerry, who was not much good at sports, wanted me to drop out of the game and play with him. He picked up the football when it rolled in his direction, and would not give it back to me. I punched him on the shoulder and he gave me the ball.

Later, he and his dad came looking for me.

"Hit him back," his dad said.

I said, "Mr. Gross, this is between Jerry and me. Jerry isn't going to hit me, because he knows that it would be a big mistake."

Mr. Gross growled and took a step toward me

"And if you lay a finger on me," I continued, "it would be an even bigger mistake. My dad would beat you into mush."

Mr. Gross drew back and left, and Jerry and I began to throw a football back and forth.

The scene shifts many years to my arrival at Fort Clayton in Panama. Most of us new arrivals had been in the Army for about three years by 1945. We had been in the New Orleans Port of Embarkation for a month, because the war was over in Europe, and the Army was in the process of regrouping. So, for about a month we would take the bus named Desire into town; and one thing that I really enjoyed was the fact that the first soldier on the bus (we were all Yankees), would throw the "Coloured" Sign out the window. The Driver would sigh, go out and get it, and put it down next to his seat. We never discussed it, but I think that the general feeling was that there should only be one US Army.

We were in a somewhat rebellious mood altogether by the time that we got to Fort Clayton. There was a feeling among the troops that the war would never come to an end; that after Japan, we would go after Russia, and so on.

So, when this Colonel got up on a platform and called us into formation to tell us that even though we were overseas — blah, blah, blah — There would be the same old chicken-shit as in the States, someone yelled "forty-eight" (a putative date for the end of the war), a bunch of guys yelled, "forty-nine," a bunch more, "fifty," and then we all yelled, "some shit!" The Colonel looked as if he was about to have a fit. "I'll court-marshal the lot of you," he shrieked. We went through the chant all over again, and he wisely got down from the platform and we were dismissed.

Anyway, a couple of days later I was dropped off at the Quartermaster warehouse, and I reported in to Staff Sergeant Andy Schmidt, a huge man who had been an All-American linebacker at UCLA. I was conscious of a strange calculating look in his eyes when he took in my Corporal stripes. "Let me show you around the Base," he said. Outside, we all piled into a truck. The Sergeant and the driver were in the cab in front, so I climbed into the back with James Stewart, the Foreman, a black Jamaican, who was also the calypso poet of the Town of Red Tank, and ten Panamanians who I was to get to know better as my working crew.

From the first, there were angry voices in the cab of the truck. I exchanged a glance with Stewart. He rolled his eyes as if to say, "Oh no, not again." I listened to the argument. It seemed to me that the Sergeant was deliberately baiting the driver, telling him to go faster, then that he was going too fast; that all Wops were lousy drivers. Then I realized why he had looked at my stripes in that funny way; he was thinking that as a

Non-Com, I would be sure to back him up.

At the first stop, we all got out of the truck. I looked around it to see what was going on. The Sergeant was about three times the size of the driver (Al Costello, I was to learn), a skinny little Italian ex-cabbie from Brooklyn, and towered over him, looking as if he were about to beat him to death, or at least bite his head off — when Costello pulled a switchblade knife out of his pocket, popped out the six-inch blade and held it out, pointing it approximately at the Sergeant's bellybutton.

"Okay," the Sergeant bellowed, "Everybody back in the truck!" We drove to the Headquarters Building and the Sergeant ran in. Shortly after, he called us into the building and led us to a conference room.

It was an instant Summary Court-Martial before a Major Thurmond, who was famous for 100% convictions in the average eighteen court-martials a month that were held at Fort Clayton.

I looked at the two opponents. The odds were about 3:1 in size and weight, and my dad's dictum came to mind. It seemed to me that Costello had shown admirable restraint, not drawing a drop of blood.

The Major called me first, after Schmidt testified against Costello. I told the Major that at the time I was too busy climbing down from the truck to see anything. He asked me what I thought was going on. I said that with all due respect, my thought would hardly even be "circumstantial evidence," and I added, "It seems to me that these two men don't get along, but the Army is a place big enough so that they don't have to be working together."

James Stewart, bless him, when he had been facing me across the back of the truck earlier, had shown his discomfort at the "frame-up", and I was pleased to hear him echo my "testimony." The Major did not bother with any Panamanian witnesses, perhaps thinking that it would waste time using interpreters, and probably realizing that even if they spoke English (which they all did, by the way), they would not be any more forthcoming than Stewart and I had been. Nevertheless, to keep his conviction average perfect, the Major restricted Costello to the Base for a week and forfeited his pay. A week later, both men were transferred to two different units.

Anyway, the men in the barracks treated me like a hero. More than one guy said that they would like to have me at their court-martials; and when Costello came by to shake my hand I said, "Hey, I was only doing what my daddy taught me."

If I may digress for a moment, the first time that I heard that line about being a big Army, was when I was stationed in the Army Building at 39 Whitehall Street. I heard it when I was passing "Tiny" Rabhan's office. He was a happy-go-lucky Corporal from Atlanta, a heavy 6 foot 8, and he wore size 16 EEEEEE boots, which arrived, one pair to a wooden crate. When one of the guys heard that Time-Life was having a contest to see who had the biggest feet in the Armed Forces, we entered "Tiny." Would you believe it? He came in second to a black Sergeant who wore 18 EEEEEEEE!

Well, anyway, when I passed his office, the Colonel in charge of the Aviation Cadet's Section was chewing "Tiny" out for making an arithmetical error on his statistical report, when "Tiny," in his amazin' Georgia drawl, answered, "Heck Colonel, whut's two men, the Army's got millions of 'em."

One of the last times that I was with my dad was when my mom and I accompanied him to Saint Luke's Hospital. He was only 39 years old, but dying of lung cancer from smoking two packs of Camels a day. He was so weak that my mother and I flanked him so that he would not fall. We traveled on the subway. We could not afford the cab fare. He placed a $5 bill in front of the cashier.

The cashier shoved it back, saying, "I don't cash no $5 bills."

My dad put his face up to the bars. He snarled, "But you could be a little more polite about it."

The cashier looked at his ravaged face. He reached into his back pocket for his wallet and said, "I'm pretty sure I can break that five, Sir."

Chapter III
MY MOMMA DONE TOLD ME

Among my dad's last words to me, he said, "You take care of your mother."

I don't know who was taller, my mom or my dad, but there was always more of her. She loved to cook and there was always a menu in our home that gave you a choice from among several days' meals.

When she found out that because I was born in December, it would mean that I would have to wait until the next winter to enroll in PS 20, she took me into the Principal's office. She started off by saying, "You mean that a kid who has already read Pinocchio and Treasure Island six times each by himself is not ready for the first grade?"

Rather than argue with her, the Principal took me into the first grade class.

One day when she was cleaning our apartment, in 1087 Simpson Street, she handed me an unopened pack of my dad's Camel cigarettes.

"Put these in the toilet," she said. "In the toilet?" I thought that I had better check. "You heard me," she said. "Put them in the toilet."

I did. And I flushed them down. There never has been much awareness of nuance in my make-up.

She went shopping, and my dad came home, very tired. It had been a very hot day to work in a letter carrier's uniform. He looked around the house, dying for a smoke, which was the reason that he only made it to thirty-nine, dying of lung cancer.

"Did you see my cigarettes?" he asked.

"Yeah, I threw them in the toilet."

"You what?"

"Mommy told me to."

"She what! Don't lie."

To come to the point, he gave me a solid spanking; my first ever. Then mom came home, and he asked her, "Did you tell Irving to throw my cigarettes into the toilet?" She said, "Why would I -- Oh my God!" And my dad burst into tears.

A year later I got my second and last spanking. My dad was saving Indian-head pennies in a big jar. It seems that they were phasing them out for replacement with Lincoln-heads, and he thought they could become valuable. Once in a while I would borrow a few, but I always replaced them, thinking that a penny was a penny. But he noticed one day that some of the Indians had become shinier and Lincolnesque. I admitted to the heinous crime and got spanked. I wiped off my tears and said, "I guess I deserve that," and he burst into tears himself.

When I was fifteen I overheard my mother telling her friend the story of how she was mugged and robbed when she was working for my great-uncle Harry, and taking the days receipts to the bank. To me, it sounded like a perfect contribution for Floyd Gibbons' "True Stories" column in the now-defunct Journal-American. I wrote it up, using my mother's name as a nom-de-plume, and embroidered it a bit. In my version, the police treated my mother as a suspect, as if it had been an inside job. According to my version, she was finally cleared when the thief made a deathbed confession that exonerated her.

The twenty-five dollar check I received was my earliest financial success. My mother endorsed the check for me so that I could cash it. I can't remember what I spent it on, but it was quite a thrill.

My mom was very handy. She enjoyed sewing for herself and others. She loved company and often had neighbors in, and as I said, she enjoyed feeding people.

My Uncle Gene loved to tell the story of how one night, after my dad died and mom and I were living with my grandparents and Aunt Rose and Uncle Abe. My uncle Gene and my Aunt Frances were driving home from Jone's Beach when they saw that lights were on in our apartment at four o'clock in the morning.

"Somebody must be sick," Frances said. "Let's see what's wrong."

"What was wrong," Gene liked to say, "Was that Rosie got up and found that Katie (my Mom) was also up, and they began to talk about food and how Rosie was dying for potato latkes, and Katie was grinding potatoes at four in the morning to make them."

We lived for a short while with my grandparents and then moved to an apartment, which had an extra room that we rented.

My mom began to go to dances and parties with a girlfriend. She was obviously lonely and looking for another husband.

I met a couple of "possibilities." When I was about nineteen, I met one guy who had pretensions of being erudite. He said that my last name was interesting, that it had two possible meanings, one good and one bad, or at least not as good. He asked me if I knew what they were. I said, "Good night," and he never came back. I wish now that I had been a little more tactful and heard him out, because no one else seems to know.

Another guy, a little younger than my mom, and a very sharp dresser, told her that if she allowed him to invest $5,000 for her, he could double it in a couple of weeks. She asked my opinion, and I talked her into letting me call the Bunko Squad at the nearest Police Station. Two detectives were waiting when he arrived that evening, and before they said anything, he began to bawl, "I have a wife and four kids to support; what can I do?"

He left with the two detectives, but they had no grounds to arrest him.

It was not more than a day or so after that incident that my mom said, "I don't see why you are wasting time going to college. Why not enlist in the Army Air Corps and learn how to fix airplanes, and then you will be able to get a really good job."

I said, "Okay, mom," and the next day I went to the Recruiting Office. I filled out an application for Hickam Field in Hawaii where they had an opening. I didn't know at the time that it was less than three years from the day that the Japanese were to bomb it. However, before I could get undressed for my physical, the Sergeant ran over shouting, "Hold it! Hold It! We can't take you; you have a dependent, your mother."

I wrote a letter of protest to the Secretary of War, Woodring, and he wrote back that since unfortunately, we were not at war, there was nothing he could do about it.

Thinking about the past sometimes brings up a lot of tangled memories. Last summer, for example, I spent a week at the Impala Motel in Ocean City, New Jersey, with my daughter, Anne, and her family. I was sitting on the porch with my grandchildren, Alison and Steve, who were flipping through some new books they had gotten that afternoon, when my memories began to press at me and I had to share them with someone.

Hoping that they would not groan inwardly, I said, "Hey kids, remember that blonde actress we saw on TV last night, on the AMC Channel? In The Three Musketeers? Yeah, Lana Turner. Did I ever tell you that we had lunch together?"

They looked at each other and shrugged resignedly.

"This was way back," I said, "In 1939, before I was in the Army in World War II, before I met Grandma Toby, before I used four years of the G.I. Bill to get my Doctorate, and before I retired from the University."

"In 1939, when I was 19, there was a depression, and I tried all summer to find a job so that I could have a few dollars when I went back to school in September.

"It was hard to find any kind of job then. I remember reading about it in the New York Times years later, in 1947 probably. They had two stories on the same page, a column apart. I wish I had saved it. I thought it was somebody's idea of a joke. The story on the left said that just prior to World War II, 10,000,000 people were out of work in the United States. The story on the right said that during World War II there were 10,000,000 people in the Armed Forces. Talk about a solution!"

The Times is such a big newspaper that things like that often slip in. Once my friend Dick Shepard, who worked for the Times, showed me a clipping which said, inside of a black-framed space, "We, the members of the New York Philharmonic Symphony Orchestra, regret the loss of our great Conductor, Serge Kousevitsky." Just below in another square, it said, "Lost anything, call the New York Times," and it gave a phone number to call.

"Anyway, someone told me to see a man who was in charge of the Jewish War Veteran's Employment Agency. They said that he might be able to find me a job, and he did. He sent me to see a Mr. and Mrs. Sturdivant at the New York World's Fair. I heard that the next day, the guy found himself a job, and they closed the Agency."

"The Sturdivants were a huge couple from the deep South, Alabama, I think, probably in their late 50's. He was very tall and rangy, and she was wide and sort of amorphous."

"They would pay me $15.00 for a 70 hour week as a shill (10 hours a day for a seven day week), not to mention that it took me an hour each way on the subway from the Bronx. I grabbed it! There were only three weeks left before I had to go back to school.

"The reason that the Sturdivants needed me to shill for them was the fact that Grover Whalen, who ran the fair, was dead set against it becoming 'commercialized.' He was naive enough to believe that the many small 'exhibits' that only existed for the sales they could make, would be content with Whalen's weird concept of the function of a fair."

The "Scientific Advance" that we were demonstrating was a gadget about a foot long. It had a black wooden handle from which an electric cord extended. A steel tube, containing a heating element, extended from the handle. Two metal plates, five inches by four were bolted to the heating element. The heat, warming these plates, would extract moisture from the air and create sharp creases in your slacks even while you had them on.

To give lip service to Whalen's wishes, the "sales pitches" were disguised as "lectures," as demonstrations of new ideas and inventions. Nowhere to be seen were intimations that the products were for sale. No price tags were visible.

"My job was to stand in the crowd, which was totally absorbed in Duke Ritter's magical performance, until he would say, 'Every man and boy needs one of these.' At this signal that the crowd was 'ripe,' I would immediately hold out a dollar bill and say clearly, 'I'll take one of those,' exchanging my dollar for a boxed presser; thus making it clear to one and all that these amazing gadgets were for sale and only cost a buck."

My action would be followed by a flurry of purchases, during which I would walk away and place the carton under my jacket. When the crowd dispersed, I would return and exchange my package for a dollar, and we would start the process all over again.

Duke would burn out four or five pressers a day, and he would disguise the fact by demonstrating that these pressers were so reliable that he could take anyone of them from the pile next to him in absolute confidence that they all worked equally well.

Within a day or two I became as proficient as a sheep dog at creating a crowd for Duke to mesmerize. I would block an interested viewer so that he would have to walk around me to see what Duke was up to. I would stand obnoxiously close to someone until they moved to a spot that needed filling, and in extreme cases I would bump into a person to get them into place.

There were always some people seated on nearby benches who caught on to my routine. They were amused by it, and they turned to others on the bench to point it out. But sooner or later they would get up and come closer only to be overcome by Duke's mastery.

I would be allowed time for a quick meal twice a day. I tried to see some of the Fair, but only managed to get to one of the larger exhibitions, a W.P.A. Art Show, which I thought was great. The funny thing is, that about eight years later, when I was working at the City College of New York, I found many of the paintings that had been in this exhibition gathering dust in the school's attic. I got them out and stored them in a more respectable place.

I usually brought some sandwiches from home and ate them at a Coca-Cola stand around the corner from our pitch.

I got to know some of the other pitch people. For example, there was this lovely girl, dressed in a bright Mexican Peasant blouse, who sold "Authentic Mexican Jewelry." It took me a few days to find out that she was Sonia Glickstein from Brooklyn College, and that she knew hardly any Spanish.

Also there were the Jolly Limeys, Ginsberg and Callahan, recently arrived from a fair in Frankfurt, Germany. They sold golden pen points for only a dollar, and the rest of the fountain pen was thrown in.

"Then one day I had my big moment, when I came close to a star. I took my lunch to the usual Coca-Cola stand and sat down next to this well dressed blonde, wearing a beige suit with mink trimming. She turned her head to look at me. She was incredibly beautiful, and she looked familiar."

"I know you," I said. "I saw you in that terrific movie, *They Won't Forget*, with Claude Rains and Edward Norris! Right?

She smiled and nodded.

"Lana Turner?" She nodded again. "I'm pleased to meet you," I said. I did not think it was the moment to mention that they were publicizing her as "The Sweater Girl," since she was wearing such a great-looking outfit.

"You were outstanding in *They Won't Forget*." (As a murder victim). "Are you in anything else?"

She smiled beautifully. "I play one of Mickey Rooney's girlfriends in *Love Finds Andy Hardy*."

I confessed that I had not had time to see it, but promised that I would as soon as possible. (Actually, I never did see it).

I could not get over how nice she was, just like a regular person. I offered her half of my sandwich, but she said, "No, thank you." I offered to show her around the fair, and maybe later around the city. She said that they were going to take some more still photographs around the fair, and that she would be flying back to California in a couple of hours.

"Anyway, I quit my job a few days later to go back to school. Just before I left on that last evening, two detectives came to arrest Duke. It seems that he was a terrific dancer, and that he and his girlfriend had just won the Grand Prize at the Harvest Moon Ball (a thousand bucks, I think). Their picture was in the paper, and his wife saw it and had him arrested for not paying child support."

"Anyway, that's the story."

Alison scrunched up her face. "Technically," she said, "You

didn't have lunch with Lana Turner."

"Yeah," said Steve, "She was already there, drinking a Coke."

"I offered her half my sandwich."

"But she didn't-" they began in unison, looked at one another and laughed.

Anyway, I did have lunch alongside of Lana Turner. I would like to read her autobiography, if she wrote one, just to see if she mentions that afternoon, (probably not). She did not impress me as a name-dropper.

A couple of years later my mother met Reuben Katz, an ex-Marine who had served in World War I, an ex-professional boxer (you could tell), an ex-cabdriver, and currently a Guard in the Brooklyn Navy Yard.

He loved to show a newspaper clipping which told the story of how, when he was sitting in his cab, he saw a policeman who was a friend, chase an armed robber into an alley, only to be shot though the heart. Ruby jumped out of his cab, ran over and picked up his friend's gun. He ran into the alley and killed the robber, only to be shot, himself. He received a Citizen's Commendation from the Police Department, but the bullet that had hit him was too close to his heart to be removed surgically; however, the story went on, the bullet eventually worked its way over to his ribcage, so that it could be removed.

Anyway, my mother married Ruby in 1942. Incidentally, he never beat me at chess. Every time he lost, he said I was a "pisscutter" (what ever that means). I did a palette-knife portrait of him listening to the radio in his undershirt It was in the Alumni Centennial Show at City College, along with paintings by Blakelock, Bill Steig, S.J. Wolf, and Zero Mostel. I was talking to the Professor who hung the Show when a group of Greenwich Village artists whom he had a lot of respect for, came over to ask him why the best painting in the Show, a "Portrait of Ruby," was relegated to such a poor corner spot.

When my mother died in 1950, Ruby was so distraught that he abandoned their apartment, and my cousin Danny, who was to become a Physics Professor at C.C.N.Y., went to their apartment to lock it up and make sure it wasn't looted. The only thing of value that he could find was Ruby's portrait, which he took into custody.

Oh yes, the point is that in December 1942, I went to the Draft Board and said, "My mother who was my dependent, just remarried, and I am yours." They almost collectively fell off of their chairs.

By December of 1942, I had been a civilian employee of the Recruiting and Induction Branch at First Army Headquarters in the Army Building at 39 Whitehall Street, for a couple of years. I had gotten the highest score on the Federal test for Messenger, just like my dad did on the Postal Exam he took. I was called for three interviews within a couple of weeks. Each time I had to compete for the job with the next two guys on the list, and each time I was called at my shipping clerk's job with Mangel's Stores, and I had no choice but to report in a grimy T-shirt and torn dungarees to compete with two guys in suits. The Navy and Marine Corps, being supremely conscious about spit-and-polish, took one of the other guys. First Army HQ was my third opportunity, and it so happened that while I was waiting at his desk to be interviewed by Warrant Officer Thurston, I saw a copy of Rabelais' *Gargantua and Pantagruel*, and I was chuckling over it when he returned. He asked me if I had read it, and we mostly talked about the book for a while and he hired me. For a while I carried messages, mostly to Fort Jay on Governor's Island, which I reached by the Army's ferry-boat, but Officer Thurston and others thought that I was being wasted, and I began to do all of their statistical reports. I didn't tell them that the Professor at C.C.N.Y. who taught Unattached 15.2 (Statistics for the Social Sciences), had given me a C, the lowest grade in 15 years, mainly because of my many absences, mainly because it was so boring.

I was still working there when the Japanese bombed Pearl Harbor (and Hickam Field, incidentally) in December 1941, and the next day all of the men in the office, except me, were in uniform.

It was a year later that my mother married Reuben and I startled the Draft Board.

My mother always seemed to worry for strange reasons. It was as if she feared that if I did something outstanding, it might call down the wrath of God upon me.

For example, there was that time when they moved me from 5A to 6A when they thought that my plummeting grades were due to boredom. It was my high IQ score that suggested the cause of boredom.

She got worried again when I took the Officer Candidate's Test close to the end of the War. It was not that I wanted to be an Officer. I had little respect for most officers, and I felt that as a Sergeant, I had the most significant job in the Army. It was just that I was beginning to get bored with Panama, and they offered a 30-day delay en route, which sounded to me like a terrific vacation.

It was a strange exam, and it still puzzles me. It was given in a huge empty warehouse. The booklets of questions were passed out to about 500 of us. The questions were not unlike the other Army Alpha Test I had taken after my induction, but the Lieutenant gave us unusual information, not once, but twice; and I seemed to be the only one who listened. What he said was that our grade score would be "the percentage of correct answers out of the number of questions answered."

My brain told me, "That means that if you answer only one question and get it right, you have a one hundred percent score." Sometimes I listen to my brain, but not always. It tends to be rash.

I thought this over and replied to my brain, "Maybe so, but this is a competitive exam. There are 500 guys taking it in Panama, and who knows how many world-wide." So my brain, which usually wants to have the last word, told me, "Okay, but take your time and do not put down any answer until you have checked it at least once." We agreed.

Everyone else, I could see, was treating this like the usual test, trying to answer all of the questions before the time was up.

Me, I plodded along, checking my answers on the scrap paper provided, and being pretty sure that I had a correct answer before putting it down.

Sometime afterwards, my Captain, Esteban Mena Alamo, told me that I had an incredible score. He was under orders not to tell me what it was, but it didn't matter, because we had dropped the atom bombs and ended the war.

Anyway, when I wrote to my mom about the OCS Test, she got very worried, so worried that Reuben took her to see the Commanding General at the Brooklyn Navy Yard, the horse's mouth as it were.

He laughed and said, "If your son even passed that exam, you don't have to worry about him. He can take care of himself."

Chapter IV
YOU'RE ONLY YOUNG TWICE

Since I have become older, my memory of what happened before I was born has become less reliable.

I know that I was the first grandchild for Harris and Jenny Goldfein, which meant that I was awfully spoiled by my mother's side of the family. I know that I was a big show-off, and perhaps a bit jaded by so much adulation by the time that my belated cousins showed up.

My father's family was more peripheral, off in the boondocks of New Brunswick, NJ and Philadelphia, PA, where I did not meet them until after my father died and I was a teenager. My Dad's sister Sarah, married a man named Zafmann and they had a boy, Dave, and a girl, Dotty, both of whom I liked very much. My Uncle Louis, my dad's kid brother, enlisted in the Army along with him and easily earned the name "Guard-House Louie," for fighting with the other soldiers who flirted with his Irish girlfriend at the Post Exchange. After World War I, he married and then divorced her, when it turned out that she was still the flirt, and he married a very religious Jewish woman and they had five daughters. I am totally out of touch with all of these cousins and miss them very much.

Once, when I was on a pass from Fort Dix, along with a Sergeant Folger who had worked in the Folger Library in Washington D.C., a library with the same name but no relation, my Uncle Louis invited us over. When I introduced him to the Sergeant who was about to sit down, my Uncle Louis who was a staunch Republican said to Folger, who was an ardent Democrat, "What do you think of that damned Communist, Roosevelt?" I left them to enjoy their three hour argument.

Meanwhile, back at the Bronx, there was my Aunt Frances, who married Eugene Greenberger, a stockbroker, and had two children, Danny and Carol. Danny became a physicist and teaches at my old alma mater, C.C.N.Y. His wife Susie is no less than the President of the American Turtle Society and was formerly a Professor of Education at Queens College. I spent a couple of nights on the second floor of their vertical ranch-type house in Bayside, Queens, listening to what seemed like hundreds of turtles rustling through their straw jungles. Danny's sister Carol married a postal worker and unfortunately they both died young. Frances was always most generous. She bought me my first typewriter, which is still around someplace because my son Matt will not let me throw it away. She also bought me my first set of oil paints. More recently, after Eugene died, I bought a set of oil paints for her to replace those she had abandoned in Miami. She was a very good painter in her own right, and showed regularly in a New York City gallery, but she has been too depressed to pick up her brushes. She is now in a nursing home and I doubt that she will ever paint again.

I often wore hand-me-downs from my uncles, Eugene and Joe, the Doctor. Their shoes were always too large, which has given me something of a fetish-complex for shoes. I must own at least twenty pairs of shoes, boots, bedroom slippers and sandals; not each, but all together.

Joe, the Doctor, once gave me an old yellow-ocherish leather jacket when it became too soiled even for golf (he was a doctor, after all), and I was so proud of it that I rarely took it off.

One day, in my Latin class at De Witt Clinton High School, I had the jacket on as we waited for the teacher to show up, when I felt something tugging at my left armpit. I turned and saw Paddy Chayefsky, the future playwright, who was cutting parallel gashes in my beloved jacket with a single-edged razor blade. We both jumped up and he lunged for safety behind his desk in the next row, but not before I punched the back of his head.

Just then the Latin teacher arrived and I sat down. He began to call the roll as usual, and the first name was "Chayefsky," who answered "Here," from out of sight, down on the floor.

My Uncle Eugene, Frances' husband, was a short, broad-shouldered, and swarthy Hungarian. He always wore dark suits with the padded shoulders that were stylish then, wide-brimmed black hats and black coats. In my movie-trained imagination, he looked like a gangster, but he was only a Wall Street stockbroker.

My Uncle Abe was kind of interesting, and I shared his room when my mother and I moved into my grandfolks' apartment after my dad died.

He was a playwright, and I saw one of his plays years later, "The Fifth Horseman," a satire about McCarthyism, performed by the American National Theater Association. It had a lot of the flavor of Giradot's "Mad Woman of Challot," together with the tang of Cape Cod accents, and it was very funny.

During the Depression he had directed a W.P.A. Theater group. His assistant was Jules Dassin, later to become a successful movie director and a McCarthy exile. Also, according to Abe, his best actor was a young kid who delivered groceries and came on his bicycle in time to steal the second act and the rest of the play. Some kid named Burgess Meredith.

Jules Dassin, alone, and sometimes with his sister, would drop in often to see Abe. Years later, when Jules was in exile in Mallorca, he invited Abe to come out there and write a script for him based on George Tabori's novel, "Short-cut." It could have been a really fine off-beat movie, possibly with Marcello Mastroiani playing the male lead, but Jules and Abe had a falling out over fees, and unfortunately the picture was never made.

My grandfather, Harris, was a staunch reader of the Forvarts, a Yiddish newspaper with, I suppose, Socialist leanings. One day I brought him a Sephardic newspaper, La Prensa (The Press), just to see what he would say. La Prensa used the same Hebrew lettering as the Forvarts, but the language was sixteenth century Spanish.

He tried to read it, frowned, and said, "What kind of a newspaper is this?"

When my Uncle Abe came home, they read the newspaper together, because he knew Spanish.

My grandmother Jenny knew several languages, but although she understood English, she never spoke it very much. She knew Yiddish, Polish, Russian, and even some Turkish words she had learned from two captive Officers who were billeted with her family and who used to walk her to school when she was a little girl.

She had a wild and earthy sense of humor, and would have a group of people around her laughing with all their might. Because her humor was so earthy, no one would translate it for me except my Aunt Rose. She told me once that they were laughing because Jenny had said that things were as cozy as "two farts in a blanket." That may give you some idea.

But I will never forget her smiling face and happy eyes. My uncle Joe, when he was interning at Bellevue Hospital, used to bring my grandma Jenny, his mother, fifty gallon jars of 100 proof alcohol, and the wonderful, ebullient Jenny would add to it pounds of cherries and bags of sugar, and put it into a dark closet to ferment to maybe 200 proof. She called the result "Vishniak," and I used to sneak into the closet and pick out the cherries with knitting needles when no one was around. They were wonderfully sweet, a bit like Irish Mist or Persian Mead, and made me pleasantly tipsy.

One day the landlord sent a painter over to do their apartment, and he asked Jenny if she had any liquor that he could drink in order to help him withstand the fumes from the paint. She told him that she had Vishniak, and she described it to him. When he heard about the cherry base, he said it sounded like "a lady's drink," but "What the heck?"

After he had downed a tumbler-full, he was so overcome that he could not even get out of his chair; and he had to start painting the next day.

When I shared a tiny bedroom with my Uncle Abe, he used to come home quite late in the summer, and he would shut the window that I had left open, top and bottom, to air out the room. In a little while after he closed it, the stuffiness would return and wake me up.

One night, before going to bed, I brought in a length of clothes-line and tied the two windows together. That night, when Abe came in, he tried to close the windows in the dark as usual, realized what I had done, and he got the idea without a word ever passing between us. In fact, he thought that it was quite amusing whenever he told the story.

He once decided to contribute a pastel painting to a W.P.A. exhibition, and he hired me with the box of pastels as payment, to help him. The subject was "The Apotheosis of Mickey Mouse," and except for the image of the great star, which I drew, the entire surface was full of nebulous color areas.

Abe introduced me to the theater, his great love. Together we saw Eva La Galliene as Peter Pan, and an unknown young actor named James Stewart, who stole the play "Yellow Jack." He had the role of a naive soldier who is talked into letting himself get bitten by a mosquito in order to prove that they were the contributing cause of yellow fever. Luckily they put an end to that peril before I served in Panama about ten years later.

My grandfather, Harris, was a magnificent carpenter (he pronounced it "carpentner"), a master cabinet maker who made all of his own tools in Poland from scratch. He made concert grand pianos at the Steinway factory in Queens. My Aunt Frances owns a baby grand she got him to buy when they moved the factory. It is a masterpiece.

When I was little, maybe four or five, he handed me a hammer and told me to hit his palm. He wanted me to see how his calluses would protect his hand. He urged me again and again, but I loved him too much to risk hurting him. He showed little interest in my artistic talent until one day when I got bored watching Dr. Joe's office and found a scalpel and a box of tongue depressors. I carved a profile on one of the flat pieces, and then carved progressively smaller and smaller side pieces, sort of like a topographical map. I glued the pieces together and stained the whole thing with tincture of iodine.

When my grandpop saw it, for the first time he said, "This kid has real talent." He understood woodcarving.

My Uncle Abe bought it from me for $5 as a Christmas present for his old piano teacher. I had become a professional artist.

By the way; even now when I work with wood to make sculpture or a piece of furniture, somewhere behind me I can hear the ghost of my grandpop laughing at my ineptitude, relative to his own perfectionism. I like to hear it, thinking that he is there and watching me.

When my grandpop retired after a heart attack, he lent his wonderful handmade toolbox with all his amazing handmade tools to his cousin by marriage, Hymie Alperstein, who was a construction carpenter. When Hymie died, shortly after my Grandpop, who died during my honeymoon (I went to the services for him), Hymie's widow gave away the tools and the toolbox to Hymie's friends. My uncle Joe, who coveted those tools and their box, was furious, and so was I to see them leave the family.

My Aunt Lil married Leo Moerman, a fellow student she met at Downtown C.C.N.Y, the business school. He sold insurance for a while and then joined Gene Greenberger's Wall Street firm. Lil and Leo had two children, Michael and Sharon. Michael, who was born on my thirteenth birthday, became an anthropologist, studying with my old buddy Mort Fried at Columbia. He also specialized in Thailand, teaching at several places and ending up at UCLA. His sister Sharon, at San Diego University, is a physical therapist who uses modern dance as a diagnostic technique. At one point, when they were still quite young, my mother and I lived in a basement apartment two floors below them.

Dr. Joe Goldfein married Irma Weinstein, a secondary school teacher (at Roosevelt High School), and they produced two sons and a daughter, who, unfortunately, I did not get to know very well since they lived in Mount Vernon.

My Aunt Rose, a sweet self-effacing person, a very talented seamstress, married a nice, pleasant, recovering alcoholic, but it was too late for her to save him.

During my teens, I continued going to school, to De Witt Clinton High School and then to C.C.N.Y. Meanwhile I was looking for any kind of job, shilling at the New York World's Fair, shipping for Mangel's Stores, and then going to work as a civilian messenger and then statistician at First Army's Office of Recruiting and Induction.

Chapter V
LA DOLCE VITA

If I ever needed proof that I was born under a lucky star, or chateau-bottled in a great year, it was my wonderful wife, Toby.

It would have bean an honor to pass her in the street and receive an answering nod or a smile, but to be married to her for forty-one years, until death claimed her, was supreme good fortune.

I always had the feeling that Toby (her Father, Dov Wiesen, called her "Taube" or "Dove"), who was the best in whatever she did, was always studying to be even better, and that she was always looking for a strategy of self-improvement.

Toby was fully devoted to our little family, and I so enjoyed her company that whenever or wherever my job took me for more than two days, I would have her take the trip with me.

She had a delightful sense of humor and could make me helpless with laughter over and over again. I will have to go pretty far to find another like her.

It was pure fate. Uncharacteristically, she went with her parents to attend a social gathering, perhaps a wedding reception, a distant family member's party, or whatever- something that as a twenty-year-old she would not ordinarily have attended.

My mother, Kate, went to it with Ruby, my stepfather, who in some remote way, was a distant relation or a friend of someone giving the party. Our two mothers were talking to one another when Toby came over to find out when her parents were planning to leave for home. After she left, Bertha Wiesen, her mother, gave her phone number to my mother. This had never before happened in history, and what is more remarkable, my mother actually remembered to give the phone number to me.

I called the Brooklyn number from our Bronx apartment, half way around the world, you might say, Toby answered.

"Hello," I said inanely, "This is Irving Zupnick, Mrs. Katz's son."

Toby covered the phone. "Mom," she asked, "who is Irving Zupnick, Mrs. Katz' son?"

"Oh," her Mother answered, "Mrs. Katz was at the party and I gave her our phone number."

Anyway, Toby and I agreed to see one another on the next Sunday; and I made the long trip and rang the doorbell.

It was answered by a vision that I was never to tire of, a beauty with lively intelligent eyes and a wonderful smile.

Overcome, I stumbled into the apartment. Offstage I heard a little girl's voice, yelling, "tell him to come see me."

Bertha, Toby's Mother, said, "Oh, that's my youngest daughter, Rosalie" (she was five at the time). "She has a little cold, and is in her room."

I went to her door and looked into Rosalie's room. Her face fell. "Oh, I thought you were Bob."

I turned questioningly to Toby. "Oh, Bob is someone who drops in once in a while and plays hide-and-seek with her. He's a real clown and hides in the closets."

Finally, as we were leaving to see Bette Davis in "June Bride," and to stop for a snack afterwards, Toby's Mother, Bertha, came to see us off. "Have a good time," she said. "It was nice to meet you, Bob."

This slip of the tongue struck me as very funny, and it took me some time to stop laughing.

When Toby returned home that night, she told me years later, her Mother asked, "Well, what do you think of him?" Toby gave her usual noncommittal answer. "He seems all right." And darling mom countered with unusual emphasis, "You will have to go pretty far to find another one like him!" Maybe she was referring to the distance from Brooklyn to the Bronx.

Toby and I met early in December, which has always been an important month for me. I was born in December, graduated from C.C.N.Y. in December in time to enter the Army, and left the Army exactly four years later, not to mention Pearl Harbor and the Day of Infamy.

We joined some of my friends at a party that New Year's Eve. They had rented a hotel suite, and it was a nice affair, with one exception.

I left Toby alone on a couch for a few minutes, and when I returned, this guy, I won't mention his name, who had a Don Juan self-image (I had met a depressed girl he had left in his wake), was seated next to Toby with one arm hanging over the back of the couch.

I went to the drink table and came back with a pitcher of ice water which I slowly emptied on his head. When he looked up at me, he saw that I was poised with this rather large cut-glass pitcher in my right hand, and he slid away and probably left for the evening.

Toby never mentioned the incident, but I think that in some way she savored it.

It was rather late when the party broke up, but afterwards, most of us went to Lindy's for their famous cheesecake. At 2 A.M. the place was packed, and the waiters were frantic, but my friend, Dick Shepard, solved the problem. As one of the waiters sped by, Dick, spotting a Greek, said something like this, "Faesuli mai faesuli, yo misi to saeculi (i.e., "Bean by bean you fill the sack"); and the waiter stopped in his tracks, pointed at us, and said, "You're next!"

We had anticipated a late evening and the Wiesens had invited me to sleep over on their couch. In the morning, Toby was up first and she woke me and told me to go into her room, because she knew that the living room where I had slept would get noisy when everyone was up. I was almost asleep again, blissfully inhaling the wonderful aroma from Toby's pillow, when I heard Rosalie open a window to shout at two of her friends who were playing in the courtyard. She yelled, "You will have to be very quiet, because Toby's boyfriend is sleeping in her bed, and his name is Irving!" No more sleep for me that morning.

Toby and I had gone to see "June Bride" on our first date, but we could only wait until May 17th; and it had nothing to do with my two hour subway rides.

Let me tell you something wonderful about Toby. We were well-suited in that we avoided controversies with one another, and with the children.

For example, from the time we met until our wedding, what with dinners out and family gatherings, I had ballooned up from my usual weight of around 175 to about 195. Toby never mentioned it, although she was always conscious about one's weight. What she did was to ask me how many times a day I went down to the City College dining hall for a "coffee break." I said that it was maybe three or four times.

She asked me how many spoonfuls of sugar I used. "Two," I had told her.

"And you have cake or cookies with it? I nodded."

"Doesn't that make either the sugar or the cake redundant? If you have one, maybe you don't need the other."

I agreed, and I stopped the sugar, and lost about five pounds.

A few days later, she pointed to the redundancy of the cake or cream. I dropped another couple of pounds by skipping the cream.

Finally she went after the cakes and cookies, and about a week later I stopped the "coffee breaks." I was back to 175 pounds.

I am not saying that we never argued or exchanged angry words; but that when we did, I was often unaware of what the argument was about; because from my viewpoint I never had any reason to find fault with her. Also, when the spat was over with, she sometimes explained it as having nothing to do with us as individuals or any direct cause. Her favorite explanation, which she had gleaned from some magazine, was that we had built up an oversupply of "prostoglandins," a word I cannot find in a dictionary, but which I assume describes an overabundance of sensuality.

The first five years of our marriage were economically unsettling, as I bumped from job to job, from New York City to Hanover, New Hampshire; to Detroit, Michigan; and finally, to San Antonio, Texas, where we had the luxury of a four years stopover. We finally returned to upstate New York with a chance to sink permanent roots in a community.

In New York City and White River Junction, Vermont, Toby had worked as a Sales Representative for telephone companies, but by the time we got to New Hampshire, she was eager to start a family. Anne, our first child, was conceived in New Hampshire and born in Detroit. This city was a kind of center for the Natural Childbirth Movement, and we attended a series of classes; but as you might expect, fate and the doctor had their own ideas, and after thirty-six hours of labor, the doctor induced the birth with an injection.

Toby said that all through her wait, she heard another woman, screened off by white curtains, saying to her Natural Childbirth Guru. "Damn you, Grantley Dick Reed! You should roast in Hell, Grantley Dick Reed!"

We were also more than a little uneasy when we brought our new baby home to our apartment, because of Detroit's medieval garbage collection system. Each apartment house had a separate concrete-block building in the rear in which the garbage pails were stored. At night, trucks rode through the back alleys to collect the garbage, spilling some as they did so, and attracting many rats. Occasionally, teenaged boys would go rat-hunting with flashlights and baseball bats, but that hardly lowered the rat population, and occasionally the newspapers reported attacks on sleeping babies by rats that had chewed their way through walls.

After bouncing through three jobs in three years of marriage, I apologized to Toby, who gave me a big lift by saying that she was not worried, because she knew that I would dig ditches if I had to, to take care of my family.

"Well, maybe," I said.

You may not believe this, but it is true. I actually looked forward to the times when my children woke up at night. I enjoyed going to them and comforting them in an effort to lull them back to sleep. It seemed only fair. Toby had them all day, and this was my big chance for some quality time with them. Toby and I never set this up as a matter of policy. It was just that I made the first move, and she was too tired to object. As a matter of fact, I once got up when Julia cried (she was our second daughter who was born in San Antonio). She was very angry at the injustice of waking up and being wet, and she looked so beautiful in her anger that I brought her into our room to share my delight with Toby. Toby, never in the rest of our time together, ever let me forget that I woke her in the middle of the night to show her our screaming baby.

Anne, in contrast, always had a high tolerance for pain. When we lived in San Antonio, our house was gas-heated by wall units that glowed when the thermostat kicked in; and in one week we found Anne asleep four mornings in a row, with her face in a book that she had been looking at in the light from the heating unit. It turned out that she was awake because of a double ear infection about which she had never complained, figuring, I suppose, that life sometimes was supposed to be painful.

Anne was very much the older sister. Once, I brought home a box of 64 crayons and two pads, and told them to share it. Later, when I looked at them, poor Julia had only a white, a black, and a gray crayon.

One summer, several years later, Toby and I spent two weeks driving from North Italy through Southern France, and part of Spain, where I was on the trail of a sixteenth-century Spanish artist, Alonso Berruguete. We left both girls at Camp Minnetoska, near Cooperstown, NY, while our son, Matthew, joined his cousins, Marshall and Glen at his Aunt Sandy's house on Long Island. We gave the girls about twenty pre-stamped airmail envelopes and a copy of our day-by-day itinerary. Probably some of the letters missed us, because we covered a lot of ground, but I still savor the six we got from Julia, and the eleven we received from Anne.

On July 9th, 1970, Anne wrote that Julie was in this year's "Miss Minnetoska Pageant," whatever that was. Anne hopes that us "guys are enjoying ourselves;" although it is "unreal" to her that we are "actually" in Europe, even though it is our third trip. "The Lake," she writes, looks beautiful," and "Today, I got to swim quite a lot lately, that makes me happy." (A true Pisces is Anne.) She didn't write yesterday, because today was Sunday, "and you might not have got the letter."

On July 12th, Anne writes that it is nice to have some other Keenan Drive girls (our neighbors) in the camp.,, Julia and Sherrie Patton managed to completely foul up on washing some pitchers; They had to wash every single one of them over!" As she writes, she is sitting on the boat house porch and "the sun is beginning to set and the water has a pinkish tint! I wish you could see it, because it's beautiful! "She thanks us for having brought her radio to the Camp, and she enjoys playing the Water Director's guitar. "Julia, Karen, and Sue love the camp; and are in the same tent! What a nut-house it must be up there! Your next letter will be in Milan! Enjoy every minute of your vacation! (Work hard!)"

July 13th — "Hello you people in Milan! What's new? Dad, did you get the information you wanted in Milan?" Thursday is her day off. (She had mentioned it before, thinking then that she might do her laundry. Now she is thinking of getting a haircut.) "I hope your weather is great! I don't want to see any more slides with you guys in your raincoats! Julie, Karen, and Sue are really a riot! Together they're dangerous! Ha! Ha! Maybe I'll get to [water] ski today! That would be great! It's about 2:00, & Dinner will have only two pots, because she [the cook] made some kind of stew! You know, she's really a terrible cook compared to you, Mom! I was so mad! I put film in my camera! I wanted to take pictures that needed flashcubes: I took the first picture. Nothing! The flash didn't flash. I decided that my battery ran out, which means this whole role of film will have to be shot outside in the day time! P.S. have fun in Milan!"

On July 14th, "Julie, Karen, and Sue were out in a sail boat to-day, which they managed to capsize! Boy, wasn't that water rough, and were they scared? But all's well that ends well. They got to safety and only managed to lose the entire sail of a brand new sail boat! Barney wasn't too thrilled!"

15 July — Tonight I start my day off! I can't wait, because that means I can sleep as late as I want!... I got back from town. I went bowling, boy was I rotten! Tomorrow I will sleep as late as possible! Have fun in Milan! P.S. I love you.

22 July "Well, how is Spain? You're really moving. Finally I got mail from you: All at once... . I told you the mail was held up Edie's been a lot nicer to me lately and all's well here! Today Mrs. Pipher dropped in to get some clothing washed for Sue! It was really great to see her! Today Julie did the last part of the beauty contest talent! She sang 'L.O.V.E.' ! You know that one that she's constantly singing! She was nervous, lost the beat in the middle, & forgot the words! I felt sorry for her! But actually, she and I both had a good laugh! P.S. Enjoy and be happy, I love you."

23 July — "I got another postcard from you today! The weather here is weird! So far we haven't even hit weather as nice as it was when I left home! It seems almost like missing summer! We have lots of fun goofing around and stuff! I enjoy being around all of the young girls! Most of them are very sweet, Julie dropped out of Jr. Life-Saving just before the test! I almost screamed! Have fun. I love you!

24 July — "I got the postcard saying you've received my first letter! That's really cool! Everybody gets a kick out of the list of places you will be! They follow you day by day through Europe with me! I'll see you in three weeks!"

25 July — "Hello! What's new? I must say you come up with some really cool jokes! (Ha Ha) Did you go into the Leaning Tower of Pisa? The postcards you have been sending are really beautiful! Pisa sure looks like a beautiful city! I got a letter from (Cousin) Jan today and it was really great! The weather isn't very nice today! Yesterday was a pretty good day! I hope you are having lots of good weather and lots of fun!"

July 26th — "I went (water-) skiing and swimming today! The water was beautiful! I skied again and fell when we were almost back because my foot came out of the ski which was too big for me. How has Spain been this year? I hope you are really enjoying your vacation and I really miss you. I saw the movie, "Mash," with all the rest of the Camp-Staff! I was the only person who hated it! Everyone else loved it! The other night I bowled a 44! P.S. I really love you."

August 2nd — "What's new" (for the tenth time). As for her own adventures, "Nothing much has really happened here, "except that "Yesterday they picnicked at Glimmer Glass State Park and had a riot playing softball & stuff."

August 4th —" I can't believe that it is really August and that most of the summer has flitted away! I don't know if I would come back if Barney should happen to send me a contract next Spring. Anyway it is hard to think about that right now, because at the moment I can't wait to get home & see you all! By the time you receive this letter you will be at your last stop before home! Have you been getting almost one letter every day from me? Like I've written? Well I love you, Anne."

From Julia:

July 12th — "At 4:00 we took a swimmer's test. Thrills? Of course, you know me, I passed. For supper we had to wash all the dishes (not only me) — our unit — At least its only twice a week —How is Europe?? I wish I could be with you, but so far I'm having fun here with Karen, Susie, and Sherry. — Only 4 people in our tent. It's great! It's not crowded at all. I'm seeing Anne a lot well, at least during meals — an occasional tongue-sticking-out contest (not really — ha-ha...) Have fun and don't worry — Next I'll write to Matthew."

July 14th "I am writing about a week ahead for each place. We just collected firewood for lunch. In a little while, Karen, Susie, and I are going sailing. I can't wait —The junior Life-Saving Class is really hard. I hope I can make it — But I'll get used to it, How is Italy? Don't forget I want an Italian wolf. So does Karen. Not really. Well — If you're pushing. Ha ha.

"I finished one role of film — I'm going to send it in. Don't forget to send me a postcard. I'm waiting for it. Matthew must be having a riot with (Aunt) Sandy and (Uncle) Chick camping and swimming. Did you have a good plane trip? Hope so — Anne goes into town Thursday. I'll give her a list."

27 July "I miss you very much. I'm having fun here though. The postcards that you send me are gorgeous: I am now in the 2:00 session. There are only 10 girls in my unit now. It's great! There are only 2 new ones. I've already used up 3 rolls of film here! I see Anne all the time here! It's amazing how well we get along in camp! (Don't laugh). I love you."

July 29th — "Hello! What's new (I'm sorry if you received no letters at the 2 hotels before this!) I've been so busy here! Canoeing, swimming, row-boating! I haven't tried skiing yet but I will try it. I don't think that I'm scared — It's just that I have no urge to do it! (Oh well). The days here go so fast! You're always busy doing something. It's fun! What have you been up to? I really love to receive postcards from you! I've received one every day."

31 July — "I have been having a marvelous time. Tomorrow I

hit a new session!!! Only 2 more weeks! It is going quickly! I'm going on the canoe trip in one week. Matthew is on his camping trip. He must be having fun. It is very warm here! It has been for the past week, but it's good for swimming. Last night we had a raccoon in our tent—Wow! ENORMOUS!!!"

August 3rd— "I forgot to tell you. Matthew, Aunt Sandy, Uncle Chick, & 2 cousins came up! They were camping in a lake near here - Today we had rain but yesterday was gorgeous! A blue sky and a nice cool breeze. Today we had to go out for an hour canoeing. The water was so rough! You'd paddle for about 10 mins. and you would be almost in the same place! Tonight we take a tippy canoe test. I can't wait — It's a riot!"

During this period, Matthew did not write, but he had some horror stories to relate about Uncle Chick's temper. He told us, for instance, that Chick was so angry at his older son, Marshall, (about Matt's age), that he threw a piece of two-by-four at him, missed, and put a dent in his own car. And then he really got mad.

Matt, as well as the girls, was happy to be home with us, almost as happy as Toby and I were to have us all together again.

Our three children are married and have children of their own now, and they and their children are all as sweet and caring as ever. Anne has two wonderful children, Steve, who has infinite curiosity and imagination, and Alison, who is outstanding in whatever she does. Anne is teaching fourth grade in the Johnson City Schools.

Julia, who met and married Gary Weston through the romantic intervention of my Renault 10, which she traded in at his car lot in Endicott, New York, now resides in Jupiter, Florida, where she helps Gary in his flourishing swimming pool business. She prepares the specification drawings for their pools. They have two awesome sons, Dante, who was six-foot-six at last count and plays football on the University of Miami team, and Paolo, the younger son, who is not far behind in size or athletic ability. Both are quite bright and also show some artistic talent.

My son, Matthew, married Stephany Gallacher, and they have a son, Evan, who has just entered first grade in Warrensburg, Missouri. Evan is very bright and artistically talented. All my children and grandchildren, show unusual artistic talent — possibly something they inherited from their superb grandmother, I guess. My son, Matthew, is following in my footsteps, teaching art at the University of Central

Missouri. Unfortunately the situation in Academia has not changed too much since my early days, and he also has been on the move seeking some sort of permanence. In his brief career he has taught to Binghamton University and Broome Community College, the University of Fairbanks in Alaska, has helped install shows at the Guggenheim Museum, and just began his present job at UCM.

As for me, nothing has ever been as important and essential to me as the warm and tender feeling I have for my wonderful Toby and the very special family that we created together.

The secret of a happy marriage is to agree from the beginning that the husband makes all the major decisions, and the wife all the minor ones. For example, the wife decides such things as should we buy a new car and which one; shall we buy a house or rent an apartment; how many children would we have and when, etc. The husband makes the major decisions. For example, what should we do about Red China, should we attack Iraq, or what part should we play in the Near East and other trouble spots, etc.

Chapter VI
SCRAPING BOTTOM

When I took my physical examination, they were still talking about the actor and comedian, Zero Mostel, who had caused a great commotion the day before, continually performing and inventing weird situations, upsetting procedures and drawing everyone's attention to himself and his comedic antics, so much so that they shot him full of tranquilizers in order to quiet him down.

I would have enjoyed meeting him. I had barely missed him at the City College, where he was an Art Major. They were still talking about him back there when I arrived at the school. I had seen him do his imaginative and highly original stand-up comedy routines a few times and found him to be remarkably funny in an almost surrealistic way.

Anyway, there must have been a desperate shortage of manpower when I arrived for my physical. My useless "lazy" right eye did not faze them at all. I think that their only criterion that day was that you should be alive, and I more or less passed.

I entered the Service in December 1942, when Camp Upton out on Long Island, New York, received 48,000 draftees and enlisted men. It was a bitter cold month that seemed to drop below -10 degrees every day. We were overwhelmed by the sudden influx of men, for which, as usual, there had been no prior planning, we were bivouacked in a shredding, collapsing, tent city; probably one that had been condemned but not torn down. Our first 72 hours in the Army was spent in continuous "Processing," without coming close to a cot until after we took the Army Intelligence Test at the very end.

During the month that I was at Camp Upton, after the rush to "Process" us, fifty-nine men died during their first weeks of "Service," mostly of pneumonia; and I narrowly avoided their fate.

What is strangest about my experience at Camp Upton is that I was so numb then that my mind refused to cope with the meaning of the needless loss to the men themselves and their families and friends of fifty-nine lives and that even today the number fifty-nine represents only faceless statistics. Maybe it is the numbness that saves one's sanity.

After the "Processing" and the Army "Intelligence" Test and about three hours of sleep, some joker came into our tent to read a list of those men assigned to K.P. that morning, and we threw him out.

The large tent that I was in, which was made up of several

smaller ones roughly joined together (you could see the stars through the gaps), was not quite heated by several tiny coal stoves. These were so ineffective that in each case, the buckets of water set next to them as a primitive method of fire-prevention froze during the night and the buckets were split in half. If there had not been a few potato farmers from Long Island scattered among us, who got up in their long-johns and emptied and restarted the stoves in the morning, the death toll would have been much higher.

After our first breakfast, we were told to exit from the Mess Hall through the door marked "To The Bull Pen." This turned out to be an assembly-point for fatigue (i.e., labor) details. I went along the first day, joining the group with shovels and pickaxes, following a Corporal who took us to frozen ground next to a latrine. The Corporal pointed out some deep crevices in which suspicious looking fluids had accumulated. He told us that the Medics wanted us to dig down to the fluid and remove it.

I took a couple of swings with my pickaxe which bounced back, making scarcely a dent in the rock-like frozen surfaces; and the crevices were from three to four feet deep.

My memory flipped to a diagram I had seen in some textbook. There it was: the "Archimedes Pump." "Corporal," I said, "Can we have a rubber hose, a mop-handle or broomstick, some tape, and a bucket of boiling water?" He nodded. "Let's get it, and we can do this job in no time," I said.

While I wound the hose around a broom-stick and taped it in place, someone poured the boiling water into the crevice to melt the fluid. Then I placed the apparatus into a crevice and began to spin it between my two hands. Exactly as the textbook suggested, the liquid climbed up the spiraled hose to the top of the broom-stick and began to flow into the empty bucket. We collected three buckets full and filled the crevice with loose soil.

The next morning I ignored the "Bull-Pen" door and went out through the other one. As I was making my way through the woods, a Sergeant from the permanent party hailed me and waved me towards him.

"I see that you are too smart to be wasted in the Bull-Pen," he said. "Get your stuff and move into the last tent on the right, and then come and see me in the Orderly Room." Temporarily he transferred me to his platoon and gave me the job of waking guys up to catch the morning trains going out of Camp Upton.

It was still dark when I made my rounds, but the cots were numbered. Nevertheless, if you did not count the cots carefully you could wake up the wrong guy who would be so sleepy that when he woke up, he might be in Fort Ord, CA or Fort Hood, TX, before he or anyone else realized that the wrong guy had been transferred out of Camp Upton, NY

Sometimes there would be two lumps in the cot, one at the head and one at the foot, and I would realize that the lump I was shaking was inert, a barracks bag, and that it was the other lump that was human.

On Christmas morning, when I got back to my 6-man tent about 5 AM, I found that all of the Permanent Party guys had left on passes. The stove was full of ashes and cold. There was no coal anywhere in the area, and no kindling. I found a magazine, "Women's Day," I think, in the latrine, and I tore off some of the wood framing from the lower part of the tent, and went looking for coal. About a quarter of a mile away, near a barracks building, I spotted a frozen pile of coal. I kicked off a big hunk and carried it back to the tent. While the fire was starting, I remember singing at the top of my voice, "I'm Dreaming of a White Christmas." When it warmed up a bit, I went to bed with all of my clothes on.

The next day I began to cough until a little blood came up. I went to the Medics for some cough medicine, but they found I had a fever and put me on a truck that was going to the Hospital.

If I had stayed in the Hospital, I probably would have been number 60 on the death list for that month. I came to this conclusion when the orderly in charge of the Pneumonia Ward took out the windows and brought them to our beds to be washed, in preparation for a rumored inspection. I decided to activate my escape plan. I had learned from another patient that if you had normal temperature three times in a row, the nurse would release you for duty. I made sure that I had a normal temperature three times in a row!

My mother told me when I called home, that some FBI men had visited her. Since I had not gone on the regular Sick Call before I was sent to the Hospital, it had been assumed that I had been smart enough to desert, but my mother informed the FBI that I had called her from the Hospital, so that the United States could breathe easier.

All of this time that Recruiting and Induction Section at First Army Headquarters, where I had been employed as a Civilian Messenger who did their statistical reports, had been requesting my return, since no one else felt like doing the damned statistical reports.

Before this request caught up with me, I was shipped by truck with four other guys into Brooklyn, where the weather suddenly warmed up, even on the bridge. I was given a subway ticket and told to report to Fort Hamilton in Brooklyn. As I made my way through the subway station with my barracks bag hanging from my shoulder I ran into two huge Russian Merchant Marine seamen. One of them slapped me on the shoulder spinning me and my barracks bag in a circle. "Dunt hurry soldier," he said. "By time you get there, Russians are already winning da war." All I could do was grin and run for the train.

After about a week at Fort Hamilton, I was again given a subway ticket and reassigned to 39 Whitehall Street, which meant that I would live at home with my folks.

I felt a little uncomfortable about that, going home every night and knowing that the neighbor's kids were all over the world, fighting the war or at least out of touch. I repeatedly asked for a transfer and was repeatedly turned down. I suspected that no one wanted to take over the statistical reports.

My way out was Sgt. James J. Leonard, a former Long Island newspaper stringer. We had had one experience together, sort of. We took two trainloads of newly-inducted, still in civies, would-be Aviation Cadets down to Keesler Field in Biloxi, Miss. Not one of us knew at the time that this group of Aviation Cadets would be quickly turned into Infantry and shipped to some trouble spot.

You might not know it but Troop Trains travel on Land Grant Railroad Lines (whatever they are), going from one junction point to another, at which time they change engines, crews, and dining cars. After the last switch in Alabama, I spent some time in an empty car swapping jokes with the new conductor who was from Mississippi. We laughed a lot at each other's jokes even though the only word that I understood was "hound-dog," and I do not think that he understood me much better.

Anyway, my trainload was made up of twitchy drunks. They got into one argument after another, over cards or dice, or any excuse whatever. Early on in the trip, which lasted two days, including a six-hour shunting to a side track while trainloads of hogs went rattling by, I confiscated six switchblade knives, newly purchased at the Hofritz Store in the railroad station, and a 38-caliber Saturday Night Special, which seems to have been a family heirloom.

Now, according to the Sarge, in his train there had been a period of silent solemnity as his young men thought of the uncertain future that beckoned, and then some one began to sing a hymn, and his guys sang one hymn after another for the same forty-eight hours that I spent in the next train.

I cannot say who had the worst of it. I guess that it was the luck of the draw, but in any case, the Reader's Digest loved the schmaltzy story he wrote about it, and paid him well for it too. Now, this Sgt. Leonard was super-Irish, a full-fledged member of the Order of Ancient Hibemians. He loved to say that with an army of 5,000 Irishmen, the war would be over in a week's time.

I loved to point out that if Ireland at least maintained its purported neutrality and stopped restocking and repairing German U-boats, that would be helpful enough.

One day the Sarge played right into my hands. He came storming through my office, which was a hallway between two larger rooms, holding a 201-file- some soldier's Personnel Record.

"Will you look at this," he said indignantly. I looked over his shoulder. The 201-File was concerned with a soldier named John Sullivan. I said, "What about it?"

"What about it? The man's a nigger!"

Without hesitation, I said, "Yeah, they'll marry anybody."

He walked into the next room. Nodding as if he accepted my explanation; and then he spun around and gave me the most vicious look I have ever seen on a human being.

Next morning I was on orders to report to Fort Dix.

I turned up in the Fort Dix Replacement Pool where I was snapped up by the Separation Center to do their damned statistical reports. Several times I had called the Major in charge of this Center to point out errors in their reports. I had been smart enough not to mention my name, and each time that the Major had asked for my name and rank, I would say, "Maybe you would prefer to speak to the Surgeon General," and that was as far as it went.

One day the Major held a special meeting. He was very troubled. "Some wild-arsed Senator (he should have been named Onager), had sounded off, promising families the Army's Separation Centers "would have their boys on their way home in only 48 hours." This was in answer to public pressure at the delays, but naturally this "Senatorial Jerk-off" had no concept of the time it took to separate men from the Service or the kind of pressure we were under. As it was, we could do the job on 800 men in two days, but the average number of arrivals was between

1000 and 1500 men a day. No one could see any way to speed up the processing, so I said that I could do it statistically by reporting an arrival average of around 800, and adding the excess to the next batch.

The Major said, "I don't understand it. Don't explain it. If you can do it, do it." I did it.

The Fort Dix Separation Center became world famous for making the dumb Senator seem almost human. The Major received a Commendation, and because of our efficiency we were made to host a conference of Separation Center personnel from all over. I shared my magic secret with other statisticians, some of whom might even have understood my methods.

A few weeks later, Sgt. Marz, who used to recite risque poems to me in Platt-deutsch (there had been a department store named Zupnick's in Frankfort before the Nazis stole it), dropped a paper on my desk. "What's that?" I asked.

"You have a ten-day delay en route to the New Orleans Port of Embarkation."

I asked him if the Major knew. Marz said that the Major had signed it.

Before I left, I turned in an accurate statistical report of the current situation, which, of course, the Major signed.

About a month or so later, when I was in Panama, Dick Shepard sent me a clipping from the now-defunct New York City newspaper, "PM," which carried the story about a scandal at the Fort Dix Separation Center which apparently took nearly a week to process men out of the Army, and the big investigation that was going on.

But before I leave Fort Dix, there are a few details worth mentioning.

First, there were the Swedes, an entire contingent of National Guardsmen from Minnesota who were included in my outfit. They adopted me as an honorary Swede, because not only had I heard of their "patron saint," Thorsten Veblen, the economist, but I had read his interesting book, "The Theory of the Leisure Class," which equated Art with "Conspicuous Consumption."

This is not the same as a T.B. coughing jag, but you know that.

The Swedes were an Army within our Army. Whenever the First Sergeant began to pick on one of the Swedes, their own First Sergeant would interrupt him and say, "If you have anything to say to one of my men, tell it to me and I will take appropriate action if it is appropriate."

I went into town with a bunch of them once, but their idea of fun was to get drunk and then punch a non-Swede. I decided to always have a "previous engagement."

Another event at Fort Dix was the arrival of Bob Basenfelder of Rome, New York, who brought with him a pile of piano music and no piano. I went to the Service Club and arranged for him to practice in private before it opened every day.

A couple of months ago (this is at least a half century later). I got curious and looked him up in the Vestal Libraries collection of phone books. He was still back in Rome, N.Y., and I called to find out if he had realized his ambition to become a concert pianist. "No," he told me, "I raise livestock on my farm."

I thought that was really impressive.

Later I became a friend of a genuine classical pianist, Jean Casadesus, who taught at Binghamton University, and was instrumental (no pun intended) in the development of the State University's participation in the Summer Program in music and art at Fontainebleau, France, about which I will have more to say later. Anyway, Jean and I got along so well because I liked him as a person without ever having heard him play- and to him, that was truly a sign of a real friendship. Unfortunately he was to die on an icy road in Canada, going from one concert to another.

I also received my worst war wound at Fort Dix, playing softball for my unit, "The Fighting (or was it Frightened), 1202nd S.U." In the first practice session I forgot that I had not thrown any kind of a ball for about six years, and without even warming up I tried to emulate my hero, Joe DiMaggio, by throwing a ball that had been hit to me in Center Field, all the way home without a bounce, as I would have done six years before. Instead the ball traveled only about twenty feet before it hit the ground and I felt as if someone had shot me through my shoulder. It was my rotator cuff, and I keep re-injuring it periodically, but probably I will do nothing about it unless the New York Yankees call me up.

Our team, by the way, was undefeated until its final game against an equally undefeated Medics Team. I usually played until the third inning, when our cook, Andy Ippolito, would run in from the Mess-Hall and take my place, and usually hit a homer his first time up. He had signed a contract with a Minor League team in the Phillies' organization.

If a ball was hit to me when I played in the outfield, I would usually toss it underhand to the nearest outfielder, who would throw it in.

The spectators thought it was a show-off trick maneuver, but there was no way I could reach the infield.

We would probably have won the Post Championship, but our pitcher, who was usually un-hittable, proved to be vulnerable to the Medics' bench-jocks, and he lost control of his temper and then his skills.

Another thing worth mentioning was the Art Program at Fort Dix. It was conducted by Professor Boris Blai and a group of his graduate students from Temple University. They would drive in from Philadelphia every Wednesday to teach and encourage the soldiers, and Professor Blai particularly liked a painting I was doing of a group of soldiers drinking beer and singing. When he heard of my interest in trying lithography, he promised to grind a couple of stones and bring them in.

The day that I was leaving for New Orleans he had the stones with him, but I had to catch my train.

"Where's your painting?" he asked.

"I dropped it off at home," I said.

"Damn it," he said. "I was going to include it in a book on Art in the Armed Forces."

"That would have been great," was all I could say.

After equipping us with parkas and snowshoes to fool the enemy subs that were prowling the Caribbean, we boarded the USS Grant, an ancient ocean-liner captured from the Germans in World War I, and in a convoy with a concrete whip and a tiny Coast Guard cutter that kept circling both of us. We took eighteen days, the slow pace forced on us by the concrete ship, to go from New Orleans to Panama.

I really hit my stride in Panama. I felt as if I was inside of a novel by Joseph Conrad. My Commanding Officer, Captain Esteban Mena Alamo, had been a Staff-Sergeant in the regular Army and received his promotion to Captain in the Reserves, before they called him up. He hated to see me leave at the end of the War, and said that I was the best Non-Com he had ever met in the Army, and he promised that if I re-enlisted he would get me promoted either to the rank of Sergeant-Major or Master Gunnery Sergeant, whichever opening came first. But I told him that I wanted to see what was going on in the real world.

He used to give me all of the jobs that he, by rights, should have been in charge of.

One time, for example, a ship full of black troops broke down in the Canal, and it was decided to let the men off at Fort Clayton during repairs. Panama at that time was under the sway of Dr. Arias, a Fascist, or rather, Philangist sympathizer who was promoting a program of "Panama for the Panamanians," a racist gimmick directed against Caribbean blacks and Asian Indians who qualified on the basis of education and the ability to speak English, either for better jobs in the American Zone, or as a kind of Middle Class of shopkeepers and businessmen.

It would have been asking for trouble, then, to release a shipload of black American soldiers into the ensuing political unrest, so it was decided to make them as comfortable as possible at Fort Clayton.

Incidentally, later on there was a rumor that Dr. Arias "fell" out of an American Army helicopter into some impassable jungle.

Anyway, the job of readying a place for the black troops at Fort Clayton fell to me. I was given a fleet of trucks, an entire infantry Company, forty-eight prisoners from the Guardhouse, and my own Panamanian crew headed by the foreman, James Stewart. I was given a quadrangle of empty barracks buildings to get ready.

We started with the wing on the right side of the quadrangle, my three groups each working separately; one putting the metal cots together in the rooms, one putting on the bedding, and one bringing in footlockers and pipe-racks with hangers for clothing. We had completed the entire right wing, when Capt. Alamo showed up.

"Headquarters, "he told me, "wants you to skip the first two buildings on the right side of the quadrangle, because they are too close to the road."

"Captain," I said, "those two buildings are finished."

"They want to leave them empty," he insisted.

"Captain, "I said, "this is hard, sweaty work, and my guys are doing a great job. I am not going to tell them that oops!, we made a mistake, or oops!, Headquarters just woke up. Why don't you go to Headquarters and tell them that it is too late to change, or better yet, forget it. They'll never come here to check anyway, and what they don't know won't hurt them. What the hell difference does it make in the conduct of the war?"

He caught on. Capt. Alamo of the Reserves was a Regular Army Staff-Sergeant at heart. Me, I felt like the wonderful Sergeant played by Louis Wolheim in the movie, "All Quiet on the Western Front." It was not the first time I had protected my men from the stupidity of officers.

One of my better days in Panama was the one in which my good friend from home, Dick Shepard, who was the Radio Operator on a Merchant Ship (the Mauna Kia?), called me on the phone from his ship as it was traversing the Canal. We did not get to see one another, but it was great fun to hear from him.

One day I visited another Quartermaster warehouse and was astonished by a man-made mountain of strange pieces of wood that was stacked in a space between two buildings. The pieces were all the same, I noted, twenty-inch two-by-fours, each with two semicircular scoops on the same side, each about two inches from the ends. In addition, each had two holes drilled about a foot apart, between the scoops. They had all been made of clean, beautiful new wood, precision-cut, scooped, and drilled. I figured it out. It was not a secret weapon. If you put the scoops facing one another, and put bolts through the drill holes, you could double-deck two Army cots with eight pieces of wood. But what I could not understand was the veritable mountain, neatly and militarily stacked, about twenty feet high, by thirty feet long, and twenty feet wide. I just had to know what this was all about.

As I unraveled the mystery, the story went as follows. Some not too bright high-ranking officer, probably from a large family, conceived of the idea of double-decking Army cots for some reason, or even no reason at all. And once he, or someone under his orders, figured out how it could be done, an order was put in to make thousands of sets of these weird pieces of wood, and for the nuts and bolts to hold them together, and of course for many gallons of paint, which were probably sitting in some warehouse or other.

Meanwhile, some other not too bright high-ranking officer got tired of signing orders for steel wool, paint removers and scrapers and fresh paint to remove the rust from the iron cots and repaint them. Instead, he put in a huge order for aluminum cots to replace the iron ones; probably unaware that aluminum oxidizes too.

Although the iron cots were phased out, another, or the same officer of high rank, ordered the iron cots to be scraped and painted at about $10.00 per cot. They were then sold to millionaire ranchers, owners of huge plantations in Guatemala at $1.00 each. These were then loaded upon Army Transport ships by American personnel, shipped to Guatemala without cost, and unloaded by our military personnel, again at no cost.

There actually were a few military operations in Panama while I was there, but I was not involved in them personally.

For example, paratroopers were dropped to silence a German-run radio station in the midst of the Great Darien Swamp, an impassable stretch of jungle, possibly the worst in the world.

In another case, six followers of Dr. Arias made the mistake of attacking a Police Station manned by Nicaraguans who killed them all. The Nicaraguans, by the way, never forgot what our Marines had done in their country in the 1920's. Therefore, we were warned never to be caught outside the Zone after dark. Because of the attack on the Police Station, we were ordered to wear our helmets, and carry carbines and gas masks at all times.

The third event, "The Battle of Panama City, "first caught my attention in the Post Theater, when the movie was interrupted several times as certain soldiers were ordered to report immediately to their orderly rooms. I recognized a few of the names. They were M.P.s and it was puzzling.

After the movie, we heard about "The Battle of Panama City."

The story was that a Navy Battleship was in need of repairs, so the crew was given shore leave, and they navigated to some bars that were usually patronized by soldiers.

What started the "Battle" was when a soldier saw a sailor take a big roll of money out of his pocket to pay his bar bill. The soldier turned to his buddy and asked, "How come they have so much money and we're always broke?"

His buddy replied, "Hell, if we done our own laundry and screwed each other, we would have plenty of dough, too."   ·

The fight was on, and it took dozens and dozens of M.P.s to stop it.

When they said "war was hell," they weren't kidding, were they?

I also managed to catch a mysterious illness after getting caught deep inside the jungle in a torrential rain. I ran a 105 degree fever for almost a month, and my weight dipped to 167 pounds, the same as it had been when I was 14 years old. Remembering the Hospital at Camp Upton, I refused to go to Gorgas Hospital, and elected to stay in the barracks; so they picked me up every day for blood tests and give me aspirins as the only medication. They never told me what was wrong, but everyone that I've described the symptoms to since, says that I had malaria. I guess I was another Army experiment.

The day that the Japanese surrendered was a continual riot, and I had the good fortune to be assigned in charge of Quarters. There was a cot in the office, but I never could leave the phone for more than a few minutes. I kept getting calls from the Guardhouse, the M.P.s, and the hospital regarding those that were sick and/or disorderly.

One of the callers was Lt. Jones from the Jungle Platoon, who wanted a jeep to pick him up at the gate. I could not get him to understand that he had the wrong number, so I hung up.

Then our huge cook staggered into the orderly room. He stood there swaying, and then finally he said, "Let's you and me fight."

I picked up the 45-caliber automatic that came with my assignment of Charge of Quarters, put a cartridge in the chamber, and said, "Which knee?"

He was not that drunk. He sat down next to me, thought for a few minutes, and said, "Let's talk about players."

I was puzzled. "You go first," I said.

"I like Gary Cooper," he said.

"Me too," says I. He seemed to run out of "players." After a while he said, "Guess I'll go to bed."

"Good idea," I said. And he did.

My last job in Panama was to inventory the Bachelor Officer's Quarters. Each B.O.Q. had been equipped with so many tables, chairs, and other furnishings such as dishes, pots and pans, tableware, etc. But during the four years of World War II, things had been borrowed and not returned, swaps had been made for one reason or another, and so on.

It sounded like a big job, but I set out with James Stewart and my dozen ready, willing, and able, Panamanians.

At the very first B.O.Q. to be inventoried, I opened the door with my master-key and we all headed through the living room-dining room areas toward the back of the house. We entered the bedroom like a gaggle of geese only to find a lovely young woman stretched out on her back, uncovered and naked as the day she was born.

We all stopped in mid-stride and tiptoed backwards through the house and into the open air. None of us had the heart for any more jolts like that on the same day. What we all thought was, what if she had awakened and found us there!

I returned to my office just in time to meet the new Commanding General. I guess that part of officer training teaches those who take over a new command to visit their territory, ask questions, show interest, etc.

This one asked, "How are things going, Sergeant?"

"Lousy," I answered.

Question 2: "What is the problem?"

I told him about the inventory (not about such perks as naked beauties, of course), about its complexities, and so on.

Question 3: "What's the solution?"

My answer was, "If a letter came from your office saying that no one could get on a plane or ship heading North until their B.O.Q inventoried correctly, missing items were paid for, and extra items were confiscated, it would solve the problem very quickly."

His eyes twinkled approvingly. "It will be circulated this afternoon."

You should have seen the activity at Fort Clayton during the next two days. That's all it took. Trucks scooting in all directions, furniture and full cartons being carried from place to place. What they did with the naked lady, I don't know, but inventorying was pretty dull after that.

We were trucked to the Pacific end of the Canal, which strangely, as far as I am concerned, is Northeast of the Caribbean end, and boarded an A.P.A. (Assault-Pursuit-Ammunition) Ship which, according to paintings on the bow, had participated in 11 landings and shot down 7 Japanese warplanes which had been foolish enough to attack her.

It was an unusual craft, very long and narrow, and very high in the water.

It was on its last trip before it was to be moth-balled, which may explain why it carried no food but chili, which was offered three times daily and had a smell that pervaded the entire ship. I ate whatever they sold in the Exchange (crackers and candy), and during my first year back in New York City, I walked four blocks out of my way to avoid a fast food place called the Texas Chili Joint.

Since we had boarded her on the Pacific end, we had to traverse the entire Canal to reach the Caribbean. I sat cross-legged on the very prow, as far forward as I could get, being eager to get home. I enjoyed the last sights, women doing their laundry, alligators, monkeys, ocelots, etc.

After exiting the Canal and passing a long breakwater, the odd design of the ship came into play in the choppy current. As we swept forward, the ship began to do great figure-eights up and down.

After a while I noticed how quiet it had become on deck. I turned around and was startled to see that the deck was empty. The hundreds of men had faded away while my back was turned. I thought that I had not heard chow-call and walked over to an open hold. I could see that no one was in the Mess except a few guys setting the tables, so I thought it might be a good idea to go down to my bunk on E-deck, below the water-line, and stretch out until chow was ready.

As I descended the stairs I found that I was on a hell-ship. The figure-eights had done their job and everyone seemed to be sick except me. Sitting on the prow may have insulated me from the universal complaint.

I climbed into my bunk on the lowest level. They were four bunks high, canvas sheets stretched to four corner posts. I took off my boots and put them on the floor just as someone in the top bunk leaned over and vomited into them. That was my cue. I ran into the bathroom. I was hardly alive when I got back, but I got all of my things and took them up to the fresh air on deck, resolving never in this life to go below deck.

I stayed topside for the six days it took to bring us to the Separation Center in Camp Kilmer, New Jersey.

The funny thing was that it was December and they had offered us winter overcoats before we left Panama., and we all said, "Are you crazy?" It was Panama after all, and why carry something that heavy?

Another funny thing was that although it was December and we were all dressed in khaki's, no one felt cold at all. But when they issued winter overcoats to us in Camp Kilmer, all of a sudden we were chilled to the bone.

Chapter VII
PAYING MY DUES

Upon my return to the civilian world, I flitted around like a butterfly to a flame for a short time, unable to overcome my fascination with any decision.

I found that my Messenger-Statistician job at First Army Headquarters had disappeared with all the people I had known there.

Gradually the realization sank in that I had some control over my life. After all, I had earned four years of higher education and other benefits, with my military service.

One day I dropped into the Art Department at C. C. N.Y. to see if anyone I knew was still around. I laughingly recalled that my dad had said, "Don't go into art; you can't make a living at it," but now I outranked him, a Sergeant to his Corporal, so what the heck!

The Art Department Chairman, Prof Albert P. D'Andrea, was shrewdly recruiting returning veterans to fill his Graduate Fellowships, knowing that the G.I. Bill would pay most, if not all, of their salaries.

He gave me a warm reception even though I had not majored in Art, but in the Social Sciences, in obedience to my dad's injunction.

And it did not bother him when I said that if I did go into Graduate Studies it would probably be at Columbia University.

About a week later I made up my mind, applying at Columbia Teachers College in the Master in Art Education Program, and simultaneously accepting a Fellowship at the City College.

The Masters took only a year, including my Summer Session courses. Meanwhile I undertook a variety of tasks at C. C. N.Y., organizing an extensive collection of photographs of artworks given to the school by the Carnegie Foundation. Also, I reorganized some very old maps of New York City, going back to when the Bronx was little more than some Dutchman's farm, while the city itself did not exist above 14th street. There was also a fine collection of W.P.A. Art.

The art included some paintings I had seen at the 1939 New York World's Fair. Several of those artists who had been unknown when I first saw their work, were doing quite well by the forties; among them the painter, Koppman, and the engraver, Erlichman.

I took the examination for Secondary School Art Teachers and received the top grades in the written and drawing test, only to fail the speech test, because, as they told me, I sounded too much like a New

Yorker.

Now, I distinctly recall passing the Education Department's Office at C.C.N.Y, either before or after I took the speech test, and overhearing Professor Jahrling's unmistakable accent as he spoke to someone in his office. These, I believe, were his exact words.

"Ve haff to keep ze speach test or else zey vill take offer ze entire Board of Education," I had already gone some distance past his Office when I realized that I was "Vone of zem!" And remember thinking that ye had vone ze var.

In one of my courses at Columbia, it was necessary to do some Cadet Teaching, and I selected my old alma mater, De Witt Clinton High School in the Bronx.

Most of my old teachers were gone, and I saw those who were still at work with fresh insight. As teachers in an all boys' school, they had adopted a rough and tumble, and sometimes a bullying, style; so that it was amusing to learn that they were softies at heart.

I was assigned to work with one of the newer male teachers. What I observed in his room was hours of chaos, shouting, and almost a physical attempt to control the students, with whom he seemed to have little or no rapport.

Finally, he offered me a block of two weeks of classes. In anticipation of this, I had found some cardboard in the supply room. I cut some of it into 16" x 20" pieces, and some strips that were 1 1/2" wide.

At my first session I handed out the 16" x 20" pieces and told the class that these were models of the acreage on which they were to build their dream houses. But first they had to design floor plans right on their "property" for the house and attached garage.

Remember that these were teenagers, most of whom had been apartment dwellers all of their lives.

We discussed some of the strategies of designing their houses, such as where the kitchen would serve best as a workroom that could observe the children's play area in the backyard, or the best location for bedrooms, removed as much as possible from street noises and lights. When the floor plans were reasonable, I passed out the strips which would be erected, with cutout doors and windows, on the floor plans, using transparent tape.

I have truly never seen a more industrious and quiet bunch of teenagers. Every day they rushed into the room, grabbed their projects and began working. When the bell rang, it was difficult to get them to return their projects to the lockers.

Other teachers from the same floor dropped in to find out what was happening. They were surprised at the quietness that contrasted with the usual shouting of threats.

At the end of my two weeks, the Art Teacher was very critical of what I had done. I was accused of "failing to motivate" the students. He also noted that I did not hold up students' projects for the class to criticize, a practice for which I personally could see no pedagogic value.

In any case, the professor in charge of the course at Columbia met with me and told me that the Art Teacher seemed to be very jealous and defensive, and that since I had caused such a reaction, he had no recourse but to give me an "A" grade.

Realizing that because of my lack of pedagogical perfection, I would probably never succeed as a Secondary School Teacher, I decided to cross the street and enroll in the Department of Art History and Archeology at Columbia University, and work for a Doctorate in Art History.

I had only taken two Art History courses as an undergraduate at C.C.N.Y In the first one, which was a survey course, I would doze off within a few moments after the lights were turned off so that we could see the images projected on the screen.

Professor George William Eggers, who was essentially a very fine lithographer, was not teaching Art History, but rather Art Appreciation. He spoke mostly about flowing lines and rhythms, and I found it to be extremely soporific.

The second course was in the Evening Division, to which I had transferred when I became a shipping clerk for Mangel's Stores. The Professor, Harry Bober, was a young Medievalist, who was soon to gain recognition as an outstanding man in his field. I have never gotten over his kindness to me, and for a young professor, his lack of egotism. I made the outrageous request to substitute a term paper on modern Mexican painting in place of the required Medieval European subject matter. He agreed that because of my full-time job and the hours that I spent on the subway, I had no time to do justice to a medieval topic, but that because I had read so much about the modern Mexicans I could tackle their work without any problem. He not only agreed to the idea, but he gave me a top grade on my paper, and we both enjoyed the memory years later when he came to Binghamton University to give a lecture on Medieval Art.

To return to my Graduate Fellowship at C.C.N.Y, I asked the Department Chairman, Prof. D'Andrea, to give me a class to teach so that I would have some experience at the college level. He promised to think about it. Imagine my surprise when I arrived a few minutes late on the first day of the next term, and he said, "You are late for class; there are eighty-five students waiting for you in the theater downstairs."

We had never discussed what course I might teach, and it was a surprise to find that it was the required Survey Course in Art History, the one that used to put me to sleep. So, with no outline and no plan, I grabbed a handful of slides and began to teach the entire history of art from the caves to what happened last week.

While the projectionist was getting his machine set up, I made some general remarks, and once everything was ready, I plunged into an in-depth analysis of Cave Painting and the society that had produced it.

The entire semester went by in the same catch-as-catch-can fashion, except for one day, when just before the lights went out, I spotted the love of my life, Toby, who had come up from Brooklyn without warning to slip almost-unnoticed into a seat among my students.

She told me later that one of them whispered to another, "He seems to be a little rattled today."

The next term, I was the entire Summer Session, teaching five Studio Courses- Painting, Ceramics, Woodworking, Metal Work, and Drawing, simultaneously in five different rooms along the same hallway.

The only course that I felt insecure about was ceramics. I had taken only one course in that medium with an instructor who admitted to knowing nothing about it himself, and I had not one complete piece to show for it. There had been explosions in the kiln, and glazes that did not, etc., but my summer students had better luck.

One day a black man from Trinidad showed up and told me his sad story.

He had come from a very poor village which was near a river whose bank was made of a very beautiful red clay. The people in his village, in hopes of developing a money-making industry, had pooled their limited finances to send this young man to New York to learn as much as he could about ceramics in two weeks. After going from school to school to no avail, he had learned that I was the only one giving a course, such as it was, in ceramics. To make things worse, he only had enough money left to carry him three days before he had to return to Trinidad.

I sent him down to the lunchroom to "borrow" a cup and saucer.. In the brief time that we had I taught him how to slip-cast the two items, and we made up a list of equipment that he could order from the catalogs that I gave him.

I only hope that things are a little better in his village through his enterprise and the little help that I could give him.

I must tell you about the Department Chairman, Prof. D'Andrea. He saw himself as a "Renaissance Man," knowledgeable in all areas of the arts and sciences. He claimed that he had "invented" the process which the Smithsonian Institute's Graphic Arts exhibition attributed to Oziahs P. Dodge who had patented it in 1875, which made it possible to transfer a color print in entirety from paper to a sheet of glass. D'Andrea was trying to get a business going with printed glass lampshades and illuminated wall hangings. But his latest craze was a newly-marketed detergent, Santomerce, which was supposed to be excellent on floors and walls.

One day he came into my painting class with some of it dissolved in a glass of water. He pulled the paint brush out of a student's hand, dipped it into the Santomerce solution and brushed it back and forth across part of an oil-painting that the student had been struggling with for hours. He slobbered a black wash across the troublesome area. "See," he told the shocked student, "Now, you're painting in temperal.

After a half an hour of struggling to remove the black smear, the student found that the Santomerce had dissolved everything including the gesso ground, and destroyed the underlying canvas.

The broken-hearted student left and I never saw him again.

I had reached the academic teaching deadline of three years, at which time, folklore tells us, you have to be given either tenure or your walking papers. Unfortunately Professor Simon Lissim who asserted that he had studied with the Russian stage designer Leon Bakst (nee Rosenberg), who died (I found out) in 1924, twenty-nine years earlier. Lissim, who also claimed to be a buddy of Pablo Picasso, was in the same boat as I was. I overheard him telling poor little D'Andrea the sad story about his Department Chairman in "Pa-rees," who had not recommended Lissim for tenure. As a result he had been so beset by Lissim's lawyers that he had been forced to resign on the same day that Lissim received his tenure.

In short, I was not given tenure at C.C.N.Y since there was only one opening (guess who got it?). As a result, I was able to devote full time to my comprehensives in Architecture, Painting, and Sculpture, and the three language exams in French, German, and Italian; and supported in the manner to which I had become accustomed by the G. I. Bill and Toby's salary as Sales Representative of the New York Telephone Company, which was located across the street from our apartment on Fifty-first between Ninth and Tenth Avenue in old "Hell's Kitchen."

Among the hurdles at Columbia were the three language exams. I passed French without any trouble, having studied the language for six years in high school and college. German was the Big Hurdle! (The bete noir or schwarze tier.) It was given by Prof. Marguerite Bieber, a specialist in Ancient Art. Hers had been the first course I signed up for at Columbia, and it was not until the second hour of her lecture that, when I caught the phrases "Ze Eyeron Aitch" and "Ze Brontz Aitch," that I realized that her lecture was not in German but English. I dropped the course like a hot potato, and two years later when I met her at the Chairman's party, she said bitterly, "you're ze vone who dropped mein course."

This conversation worried me. She had even failed one of the students who had studied for two years at the University of Stuttgart in Germany. His mistake had been that he had neglected to take the unofficial translation course given by Prof. Bieber's housemate, Marguerite Muesam, whose lack of familiarity with English sometimes caused confusion. I once translated a phrase which, I thought, said that something was "like" something else, and she said, "No. No. Ziss is similar unto zat."

Anyway, I credit a hysterical seizure by a sweet and usually happy-go-lucky girl from Texas. She threw a fit outside the Office of the Chairman, the eminent Archeologist, William Bell Dinsmoor, who came out to see what was causing so much noise. Just in time he caught a small sarcophagus which had been toppled from its pedestal by one of the young lady's errant kicks as she threw herself about on the floor, weeping bitterly. When he found out that the cause of her anguish was her third failure in the German language test, he announced that there would be a change made "directly."

The innovation announced by Dinsmoor's office was that now you could have a choice between Professor Bieber or Professor Julius Held. I decided to opt for the latter as soon as possible.

The exam was relatively reasonable for German, and I felt that I had handled it well. I went to his office to find out how I had done, and

Held was just saying, "You did not do badly, but I sink you should take it vone more time for ze experience," when Prof. Meyer Schapiro, who shared Held's office came in. "Is this that stupid German Exam?" Schapiro asked. "I think its absurd to hold up a promising student like Zupnick for that ridiculous exam, when he could make better use of his time doing something else."

Held's reaction was incredible. First, the color drained out of his face completely, making it look like an ivory carving; then reds and purples washed over it.

"Ven vould you like to take ze re-exam?"

"Tomorrow," I said.

"Tomorrow!" he shrieked. "Don't you sink you should study a little more. A veek or two?"

"I don't think that studying would help me translate any better than I did on the last exam." I took it the next day and passed. I had assumed that he would be too embarrassed by Schapiro's remarks to do anything but pass me, and I was right.

Not that Schapiro was always helpful. For example, it took me eighteen months to do a term paper for him on what was universally acknowledged as "nonexistent" Romanesque Sculpture in Provence before the construction of the Church of San Gille. He kept insisting that there was something; and when I finally turned in my paper, he brought out a publication of the Auto Club of Auvergne and showed me an illustration of an undated and unsculptured floor slab with an incised outline representing a local Saint.

But what was worse was that he included a trick question on my Architecture Comprehensive, something about the Saracen "impact" on Norwegian Church Design, just because "I wanted to see what you would do with it." Luckily I was able to pass the exam without answering his question.

As a result I was happy that he was out of the country when I defended my Dissertation.

I had my revenge on Schapiro some sixteen years later, in 1966-1967, to be more exactly, when I published "The Mystery of the Merode Altarpiece" in the *Burlington Magazine* in London, refuting Schapiro's article, "Muscipula Diaboli, the Symbolism of the Merode Altarpiece," in the Art Bulletin, on the same altarpiece which is in the Cloisters Museum in New York. Schapiro had asserted that a strange-looking object on the window of St. Joseph's carpentry shop was a mouse-trap, symbolizing God's use of St. Joseph's son, Jesus, to trap the devil. I argued that the object on the window-sill was a primitive form of carpenter's plane, not unlike some used in rural Pennsylvania early in the nineteenth century.

Schapiro countered with a note in the *Burlington Magazine* purporting to show mousetraps depicted in a very old Hebrew Manuscript.

My "Victory" came in 1967 when an English Translation of Max J. Friedlander's monumental, seventeen volume *Early Netherlandish Painting* was published, just too early to include Schapiro's note in the bibliography, but just in time to give me *the last word.* So there, Meyer!

Chapter VIII
A GALLOP IN THE FIELDS

I set new records taking the three language exams and three comprehensives in less than ten months, but it was eleven years after I entered the program before I defended my dissertation and received the Doctorate. More about that later.

In a course in Baroque Are, Prof. Rennselaer Lee, my first dissertation advisor, went into a sort of fugue one day during his lecture. Somehow he got into the topic of the Jesuit Order, repeating all of his New England WASP-ish prejudices about them. After about five minutes of his harangue I became embarrassed for him, and stood up. "Sir," I asked, "Is this relevant for the development of Baroque Art?" He shook himself, and then returned to the planned subject of his lecture.

Afterward, a fellow-student, whom I had not met before, Mark Peisch, came over to thank me for interrupting Professor Lee, and we later became close friends. Peisch was a Vermonter and a Catholic, living in darkest WASP Country, where he said, the closest Church was 50 miles away, and their neighbors treated them like Jews in Germany.

It was Mark Peisch who recommended me to Dean Morrison of Dartmouth College when they were looking for a substitute for an Art Historian who had just had a gallstone removed. The Dean offered me one semester, but I said that it would not pay for me to move for less than a full year. The Dean agreed and even mentioned the possibility of a tenure appointment in the future.

Toby and I packed our meager belongings into cartons, called the movers, and left with two suitcases. The irony about the Dartmouth job, when you think about the events that led to my hiring, occurred during our first week on Campus when Toby and I were invited to a party meant to introduce us to the Art Department. During the first hour of the party one of the Professors began an anti-Semitic joke about C.C.NY and the Chairman, Prof. Hugh Morrison came over just in time to grab my right arm and say, "Zupnick is Jewish, you know." What I knew right then was the fact that the Dean's mention of tenure tracks had little meaning in a school in which such decisions depended upon a unanimous vote.

Dartmouth had a Belles Lettres Society at whose meetings newer faculty members, usually, were given a chance to show their potential by reading a research paper. I had just finished writing a paper on "The

Aesthetics of the Early Mannerists," in which I attributed the abrupt change in style in the early Sixteenth Century from Renaissance Realism to a more abstract, formal and decorative style, as a reflection of the growing interest in Neo-Platonism shown by the members of the Medici-fostered Platonic Academy of Florence.

After I finished reading my paper, a spirited discussion flourished; some professors told me, "the most exciting and interesting" that had taken place after any of the earlier readings. What bothered me, though, was that the give and take of the discussion had little or nothing to do with my paper. Evidently, no one had really understood it.

When I got home and told Toby about it, she asked to read the paper. "No wonder," she said. "It's too wordy and convoluted. I'm reading it, and I can't understand it." She got me a pad and a pencil, and we went over the paper sentence by sentence. She would say, "What does that sentence mean?" I would explain it to her, and she would say, "Write it down that way."

Afterwards, I rewrote it several times until she said it was good. It was to be my first scholarly publication and the first paper on Mannerism in the Art Bulletin ; thanks to Toby.

After it was published, my Chairman, to whom I had sent an offprint copy, came into my office and asked, "What is Mannerism? They never taught anything about Mannerism in Princeton. "Well," I said, "What can you expect from such a backwater University?"

I don't think he got the joke.

I published two more papers that year, probably more than the entire faculty at Dartmouth over a ten-year-period.

Dartmouth's library had a wonderful mural by the modern Mexican artist, Jose Clemente Orozco. To my mind it was a spoof on higher education. One memorable section shows a group of academics, identifiable by their robes and mortarboard hats, dissecting a skeletal corpse. Orozco's colors are so powerful that they impinge on your concentration, which might have explained why none of the faculty or students can ever be found in the library. I was inspired by Orozco and other contemporary Mexicans to do a painting called "The Generals," which shows a group of generals dissecting a map.

Several faculty wives, all "Smith Girls," came to our apartment. Most of the faculty are former Dartmouth students; you should understand, and many Dartmouth students visit Smith College, which is not far away, looking for dates, and as a result, frequently marry women from that college.

As the faculty wives entered our apartment, one of them shrieked when she saw the painting (Toby gave a great imitation), "WHOT IS THOT?" She exclaimed. Toby, not wanting to embarrass her, said, "It's one of Irv's latest paintings. Isn't it interesting?" The Smith Girl said, "But NOT in the LIVING ROOM!"

General Eisenhower, running for President, came to Dartmouth to give a campaign speech, surrounded by bodyguards. He need not have bothered. An earlier political poll on campus showed 99.7% Republican. Probably, Toby and I accounted for the "other."

Because of my background, I was asked to teach a community painting course. I was to charge each member of the community a small fee, and since Dartmouth had no studio program I was to allow students to attend without charge. Paul Sample, the Artist-in-Residence, was listed a as a Faculty Member, but he was not to be bothered with such petty considerations

One of the students who attended my painting class, had an un-usual background. Coming from Hawaii, he had been made an Honorary Member of the National Academy of Science at the tender age of twelve, for his discovery of several heretofore-unknown sea-shelled species. He was a brilliant student in several areas, and turned out to be a very talented painter.

To my astonishment, the Chairman came to my office one day and asked about this student's painting. After I raved about him, the chairman said, "I have had second thoughts about him. Mostly he is here because of my recommendation, and I might have made a mistake."

"What!" I shouted. "This guy is outstanding in nearly everything he does. You should be proud to have recommended him."

"Well," said the Chairman, "He's not interested in sports or group activities. He's a loner and not at all well-rounded." I was stunned until I remembered that the Dartmouth Catalogue said in clear, perfectly and unabashedly legible print that it would have turned down an application from Albert Einstein (not because he was Jewish), because he was not well-rounded.

Well, Toby, who had never painted in oils before, attended my class and with no hesitation did one fine painting after another, and she was more wonderfully rounded than anyone I was ever to meet. And I know in retrospect that she was responsible for the outstanding artistic talent that appears in all of our children and grandchildren.

Then, there was an eighty-year-old woman who put Grandma Moses to shame.

She came to my painting class one night, carrying a paint-smeared tin artist's box. She said to me, "I been paintin' tole-ware, you know, tin stuff with lambs and flowers and so forth, and I'm damned tired of it. Could I use the same paints and brushes in your class?" I checked them out and nodded, and she took a seat behind an easel and began to paint from the model, a local carpenter who was posed as if he were sawing wood.

A half hour later I checked her out. She had diluted her paint with so much turpentine that her picture looked like a water color. I sat down and briefly discussed her painting as an example of a "Linear" style (Flat, smoothly textured, and with areas carefully filled in to the outlines of each plane). I contrasted this with the *possibilities* of a "painterly" style in which the texture of brush strokes and the free assemblage of forms play important roles. An hour later, she was painting like Ensor and Van Gogh rolled into one.

Two weeks later she asked me where she could have a one-man show; and she invited Toby and me to come over to her house and see what she had done.

So, on a very snowy night, with minimum visibility, she drove us to her house, cutting across sidewalks and open fields. Toby sat next to her in the little Volkswagen "Beetle"! The woman's daughter who was engaged in bio-chemical research at Dartmouth, and I, crouched down behind the front seats. The rear seats had been removed, I guess, to make room for groceries or paintings.

Her house had a triangular floor-plan, fitting into one corner of a commercial garage lot. A Civil War cannon and a pyramid of piled cannon-balls were in front of the house, and the interior was decorated with Civil War memorabilia; uniforms, swords, rifles, and banners hung on the walls- along with 45 terrific new "painterly" oil paintings, which she had done in only two weeks!

Grandma Moses, humph! My student was an "old master." She finally arranged shows in her Church and the town Library, and she sold very well.

I have three other memories of Dartmouth that I treasure. The first has to do with the ancient electric stove that came with our apartment. I was not surprised to see it later in a museum in Detroit, where it was labeled as the earliest electric stove ever produced. Ours, at

Dartmouth, would cook on one side of a frying-pan, and you would have to turn it 180 degrees to finish the other half of omelet. I mentioned this problem to someone in the Business office, and they said that it would be replaced.

One day there was a strange racket coming from our staircase. I looked down into its four flight abyss and saw two men carrying up our new stove. Finally, they managed to get it into the kitchen without creating any appreciable damage.

They stood there, panting and looking at the old, dysfunctional stove. One of the men was close to sixty; the other in his early twenties. The younger man finally said, "You reckon that there stove's as heavy as the one we just brung?" The older man digested the question for about three minutes twisting the lower part of his face in a variety of configurations.

"Cinch taint no lighter," he snapped, and they left the two stoves standing side by side. A couple of days later the electrician showed up and unplugged the old stove. "Got to put new wirin' in for the new one," he said. He pulled the old wiring out through a hole in the wall after removing the outlet, and then he shoved some fresh wire through the same hole. He turned to me and said, "Would you hold this end of the wire and see it don't go down the hole?" I held on to it as he ran down four flights of stairs into the basement. His first tug almost pulled me into the wall.

A couple of days later the first two guys came for the old stove. I'm sorry I missed that.

The second memory has to do with a memo from the English Department asking for a list of students with writing problems. This was in *1952-53,* and many of these students had been in schools disrupted by the absence of their teachers in World War II, and by the advent of something called "Progressive Education," or "Don't sweat it!"

I had listed about *35* students, and the English Department called me. "You listed *35* students with writing problems," it said, accusingly. "I believe so," I replied, "Do you realize that eight of them are supposed to graduate at the end of this semester!" I said, "I guess that you and they have a problem."

My third fond memory has to do with the arrival of the Saddler's Wells Ballet Troupe from England. They had come to perform "Swan Lake." Some local farmhands help set up the scenery, and the Director saw this one old fellow gaping at the girls who were exercising on the bar.

"What do you think of them?" he asked the old farmer.

The old man shook his head. "Limber folk, ain't they?" he replied.

Being fully aware that my days at Dartmouth were numbered I took an examination for the job of Educational Curator at the Detroit Institute of Art. The exam was given in Boston and New York City. I took it in Boston along with Graduate Students and Professors from Harvard, Yale, Brown, and Boston Universities. In New York the competitors were from Columbia University, NYU's Institute of Fine Art, and Fordham and Princeton Universities. Being relatively fresh from my Comprehensives, I came out first, was interviewed in New York by William Woolfenden, my future Department Head, and hired. Toby was pregnant with Anne, our first child, and I packed everything else, and we headed West.

All this, only to find that I had been hired to hold a position open for someone named Bobby who everyone loved, and who was spending a year at the Brooklyn Museum so that he could take advantage of a loophole in civil service regulations and earn a big jump in rank and salary.

To everyone I met, I was the guy who was "using" Bobby's office. I also learned soon enough that as a married man with a pregnant wife, I would never be in the inner circle. The Guards and Carpenters and Gallery Technicians, would ask me incredulously, "How did you ever get hired to work on the Curatorial staff?" My future was handwritten on the wall.

I shared an office (using Bobby's desk, of course), with a man who had at least three personas. With me, he was gruff and macho. When he spoke to his Mom on the phone, once or twice daily, he was so deep-South you could smear his words on cornbread. When he was with the other curators, I would catch jokes such as, "Oooh, my girdle's too tight!"

I didn't mind all the gaiety, but I had no desire to share in it. It was a little depressing to be the one who could see in the land of the blind; or is it vice versa? Actually it was not as bad as being surrounded by a swarm of WASPs.

A group of dentists' wives hired me to teach them outdoor landscape painting on Saturday afternoons. One day, four of their husbands, all dentists, came along.

In the course of conversation they asked me for the name of my dentist.

"Dr. Perdue," I told them.

They all laughed, because they all had studied under him in dental school.

"You know what his nickname was?" one of them asked. "Couldn't guess," I replied.

"We called him Pooh-pooh. Get it? Pooh-pooh Perdue."

Among other activities, I participated in a weekly series of lectures which used slides, and which was followed by a tour of the relevant part of the Museum Collection. I was assigned Ancient Roman Art, about which I had a minimal background. I concentrated upon the positive achievements of the Romans which distinguished their contributions from their Greek predecessors; their use of concrete in domes and arcades, their building of roads and bridges, and the realism of their painting and sculptures. Woolfenden, my mentor, told me later that I was speaking over their heads. I said, "How come so many of them came up later to thank me for not treating them as if they were twelve years old?"

I was given the mummified hand of a fourteen year old former Egyptian Princess to show the school children. It was a beautiful hand and wrist, suggesting someone dainty and precious.

One day, another curator asked me if I could lend him a hand. "Sure," I said, and I took the Princess's hand from my desk drawer and offered it to him.

Somehow, the story appeared a day later in the *Detroit Free Press*. It must have been a slow day for news.

As Curator, I was put in charge of the McPharlin Collection, which consisted of a fine theatrical library and a wonderful collection of puppets and marionettes. Detroit is the headquarters of the Puppeteers of America Guild, and I soon engaged some local puppeteers in restoration work. They were actually thrilled to handle these historical masterpieces. My chief responsibility was to exert extreme caution to prevent them from over-restoration, and to make the Guild members realize that some deterioration over time was important evidence of a puppet's or a marionette's long existence. It was also difficult to pry the Guild Members loose when it was necessary to close the Museum.

I was also offered an hour's time on the Institute's regular Television Program, in order to advertise the McPharlin Collection.

I took this opportunity to write a playlet about "Judith and Holofernes." One of the Guild's puppeteers performed admirably, while I took care of the scenery. In this "little" playlet, I showed the significance of three items in the Institute's Galleries, bronzes by Brunelleschi and Ghiberti, and a wonderfully hideous painting by Orazio Gentileschi, a woman who could hold her own with any master of the Baroque style of the Seventeenth Century. In my research on Judith, I was astonished to discover a handbook written to teach nuns "The Ancrene Rewle," first printed in Middle English about 1450, which in four or five places urges the nuns to follow the example of Judith's self-sacrifice to save the Israelites. She is the only woman put forth as an example to the nuns in this book, which does not go into the other details of the story in which she throws herself at Holofernes, who takes her into his tent, where she gets him so drunk that she can decapitate him in order for her people to demoralize the enemy by displaying his head on the Israelite city gate the next morning.

In my playlet, a boy asks his mother about Judith, and she asks a Guard, who relates the story. I solved the beheading scene by having Judith and her victim enter a tent which shakes violently as dramatic music plays in the background and Orazio's painting makes it all clear.

One of my tasks as Curator of the McPharlin Collection was to set up a demonstration of a group of Mid-Nineteenth Century marionettes which had been used to entertain people in the gold-mining camps and throughout California. The piece-de-resistance was a breakaway skeleton, which had arrived as a shopping bag full of wooden bones, a carved skull, and shredded wispy bits of twine attached here and there to the wooden pieces. I had never seen such a marionette, which could suddenly grow to a much larger and scarier size right before your eyes. It seemed to me that this marionette could be the focus of my demonstration.

I bought some twine and in a few hours of feverish concentration, I was able to demonstrate the new attraction to rave reviews.

Our first child, a daughter, was born in Detroit, and I drove Toby to the Hospital at 3 A.M. during the worst blizzard (three feet deep) in the City's history. I received a parking ticket during the three minutes that it took to walk Toby to the Recorder's desk.

It was a couple of months later when I was officially informed of the pending arrival of Bobby. In their own eyes the administration was quite humane about it. They knew that It would be unlikely for me to find an academic job at such short notice; so, if I agreed, they could have me transferred at the same grade and salary to the Department of Parks and Recreation. Not having much choice if I were to take care of my family, I accepted their generous offer.

For a few weeks I ran an arts and crafts program at a group of libraries. I came up with the idea of running a miniature soap-box Derby, with small wooden cars, using checkers for wheels to roll down portable ramps. I would make the car bodies, the kids would paint them, and I would nail on the wheels.

To get supplies, I went to the closest lumber yard and asked if there were any scraps that I could buy (I could sell them to the children for a few pennies).

The counterman said, "Buy them? You want to buy them? Wait here!" He sped of into an office and came back with the owner.

The owner said, "This is a first. The other guys always want free wood, so I never have any. You come back tomorrow. We're cutting a big job, and I'll fill up your car- FREE!"

And he did. I could hardly see where I was driving.

Unfortunately, I never got to use the wood for my project because school was finished and the summer begun, and I was reassigned to take over a schoolyard in the deepest slums in Detroit, between a black neighborhood and a neighborhood of southern whites, during the usual depression in the auto industry. This schoolyard had seen an average of two riots per summer for six years in a row.

My supervisor, looking at me as if I were about to be thrown to the Detroit Lions, suggested that before I report to my schoolyard, I should talk to another employee who worked at a nearby school. "He's been doing this for years, and he can show you the ropes."

I found the guy who was to be my mentor. He was wearing an Army Issue helmet-liner and carrying a four foot long wooden club with barbed wire nailed to the upper end. He demonstrated his philosophical approach. "I keep my back to the wall and I don't let nobody get closer then that." He swung the club back and forth in an arc.

"Oh," I said.

When I arrived at *my* schoolyard, I found it to be full of black children with a few white ones sprinkled in. A man was waiting for me to sign a "receipt." On this piece of paper I found a description of the location of the only unbroken window to be found in the school one day after it had closed for the summer.

The man explained that it had escaped vandalism because it was hidden behind a projection of the building. I signed the "receipt." The Department of Parks and Recreation would henceforth be responsible (meaning that I would) for the surviving window and the other windows as they were replaced.

I turned around to look at the yard. A tall, lanky black man with snow white hair was pitching a soft-ball game for two mixed teams of boys and girls, white and black, who ranged from about six to ten years in age.

When he saw that I was finished signing the "receipt," he came over to introduce himself. He was Tom White, my janitor, and he was ready to do anything that I thought needed doing.

I said, "You are doing great. You're taking care of eighteen kids. I can't think of anything more important."

He gave me a set of keys and pointed to a wooden door in the courtyard. I went over to it, and opened the door, and looked in. It was a small room, almost filled with a huge cardboard carton in which I found a pile of games and a smattering of sports equipment.

Suddenly a black boy stuck his head under my arm. "A basketball," he said, "A basketball. You got a basketball?"

"Yeah," I said, reaching in to get one. He whisked it out of my hand and dribbled it out into the courtyard.

I guess I should have had him sign for it, I thought, and then remembering my own boyhood, I realized that probably no one would ever find him.

But I felt much better about it when I came out to find a basketball game in progress. It seemed to be a very exciting game even though there was no basket but only a magic spot on the cyclone fence.

"Isn't there any basket?" I asked one of the Subs.

"We had one last year," he said, "But somebody stole it and we ain't had one since."

That bothered me. There was all this spirit and hustle and no equipment to authenticate the experience.

Using the keys, I went down into the basement where I found an empty, broken wooden barrel.

I kicked out the wooden slats and took the two metal rings which I fastened to a piece of plywood. I drilled holes in the corners and threaded some wire through them to give me something with which to attach it to the fence.

I returned to the schoolyard dragging a twelve foot folding ladder and my basketball hoop and backboard.

The game stopped and the players looked at one another as I opened the ladder and dragged "the equipment" into place and fastened it to the fence. At the moment I finished, a basketball arced over my shoulder and through the hoop.

My handiwork lasted about thirty minutes, and I returned to the janitor's workshop, accompanied by Jerome, the lad to whom I had given the basketball. There I found some heavy strap iron and a half-inch thick plywood square. Together we forced the iron into a hoop and fastened it with nuts and bolts.

This time the players opened and set up the ladder. They handed the contraption up to me, holding the ladder so that it would not shake.

Again, as soon as I finished hooking it to the fence, a ball swished through the basket.

This one lasted an hour and a half.

A little while later the Supervisor showed up, to come and see if I was still alive. I was, and I was bristling with anger.

"You see that hunk of plywood on the fence?" I asked.

"Yeah?"

"Well, tomorrow morning I want to see a real basketball hoop and backboard hanging right there."

"Well," he said, swallowing, "I'll have to check the budget, get a requisition, and submit it to finance."

"You are not listening," I told him. "Tomorrow morning I'll drive up in my little black Chevy. If I don't see a basketball hoop and backboard then I'll go home sick, or whatever, and you can watch this playground."

Next morning it looked as if they had raided Madison Square Garden. The importance of proper motivation should not be overlooked.

The game was already on, because i had not seen any purpose in locking away the basketball every night. It was life's blood to my players.

"About that basketball hoop," several of the players came over to tell me, "You don't gots to worry about nobody stealin' it. We's gonna have guards sleepin' here every night."

A wonderful heart-warming bonus emerged from that basketball hoop.

A series of games were played every other afternoon between *my home team* and a team of white newsboys who arrived on a fleet of bicycles after making their deliveries.

I have never seen cleaner, more sportsmanlike games in my life. There was no referee. Players would call fouls on themselves. They would say, "Oops! My foul. You get two shots." Just like that.

My assignments varied from week to week. I guess that I was a kind of universal sub. Sometimes I was in charge of the Municipal Shop, which was open to the people of Detroit so that they could build or repair furniture.

One day when I was assigned to Belle Isle, a recreation park in the middle of the Detroit River, I listened to a lecture by a tipsy football coach on 12 ways to "bust" an opponent's nose without drawing a penalty. He summed up by saying that "once you bust a guys nose, you don't have to worry about him coming back in the game."

I also worked at a Recreation Center, and occasionally in High School gyms.

One night I will never forget, I was closing up Cass Tech's Gym and I found three basketballs on the court. Too many to carry all at once. I picked one of them up and threw it overhand to the end of the court to get it closer to the door. To my surprise, it swished cleanly through the basket, about fifty feet away. It was maybe the third time in my life that I had made a basket from any distance.

Three little black boys stopped in the doorway just in time to see my accidental basket. Their eyes looked enormous. "Wow!" One of them said. "He must be somebody!"

Shortly thereafter I read that the U.S. Army was looking for Arts and Crafts Directors at Army Bases and paying *50%* more than I was getting in Detroit. I sent in a letter of application, and the return letter from Washington, D.C. asked me to meet the Program Director at a meeting she was conducting at Michigan State University in East Lansing

Toby and I and our new little daughter, Anne, went to meet the Program Director. She said that she might be able to offer someone with my qualifications and experience something even better than a Post Directorship.

The next communication from Washington offered me a position at Fort Sam Houston in San Antonio, Texas, the headquarters of Fourth U.S. Army, in which I would be developing a program at fifteen Army Bases in a five-state area (New Mexico, Texas, Oklahoma, Arkansas, and

Louisiana), at double any salary I had made until then.

We accepted without hesitation, and my little gypsy family was on the move again, in our less than willing Chevrolet.

Chapter IX
FROM TEXAS BACK TO THE US OF A

We were to spend four years in San Antonio, and I guess that if it were not for the caliche soil (I'm joking) and my mad impulse to finish the Doctorate in Art History and Archeology I had started, and to put it to good use in some college or university, we might have put down our roots there.

About the Caliche soil. After renting an apartment fairly close to Fort Sam, where my office was, and living there for several months, Major Metzgar convinced me that I was throwing money away, that in Texas when you paid your "earnest money" on a house, they gave you the keys; and that instead of never seeing my rent payments again, I would earn "equity," as I paid off my G.I. mortgage.

We bought a nice little house, 315 Cresham Drive, very close to Fort Sam. Each house on its clean quiet street had a young five foot tall maple tree in the center of its front yard. When we moved in, there was no grass except for little tufts of Saint Augustine, about eighteen inches apart. In a few months I could only mow a few inches at a time with my old-fashioned push mover, after backing up about three feet and charging at it. That was tough grass. It snaked along underground and came up in several places at once. I had to buy a machete to defend the flower-boxes.

One day as I drove home, I noticed that one of the maple trees that had been planted by the developer in front of a corner house, had lost all of its leaves and for no apparent reason, died. The next day, two more trees had died, one on each side of the street. Every day I saw another casualty, or two, or three. I fought for mine gallantly -extra water- various fertilizers, intravenous injections, oxygen, etc.

What was the answer? Caliche, an alkali soil. Once the roots of a plant or tree touch it, they die. The desert takes over.

The defense? When you plant something, you dig a big hole and coat it with powdered green copper sulfate and then refill the hole with topsoil from someplace else.

Before I left San Antonio, I had planted fourteen flourishing trees. My little daughter, Anne, complained. "Don't plant any more. We won't have any place to play in."

By "we," she included her younger sister, Julia, who is our native Texan. One day Toby looked into our fenced in back yard and panicked. Both girls were gone!

She ran outside, noticed that the gate was unlatched and ajar, and she ran out into the fire lane that ran off into infinity in the flat Texas landscape. A hundred yards away she made out two square diapers enfolding two little girls who were walking off into the sunset hand-in-hand.

My first week as Director of Fourth Army's Arts and Crafts Program, part of Special Services, which also included Sports, Music and Theater, Service Clubs, and Libraries, was hectic to say the least. I arrived on a Monday and met my colleagues: Colonel Boswell T. Ulmer, the Special Services Officer in Chief, the Director of Libraries, Helen Frye ("Don't make any jokes about my name"), and the others. Later I was to recruit Doc Naylor, a musicologist who had directed the Cincinnati Conservatory of Music and chaired the Music Department at the University of Alabama. He wanted to be in Texas, because his daughter, another Doc Naylor, was teaching music at Baylor.

The first thing I was told was that I had $80,000 in my Arts and Crafts Budget, and that I had until Friday to spend it, or my funds would be severely cut in the next annual budget.

I busied myself, reading reports from my fifteen programs in our five state area. I was looking for something expensive to buy for the program, which included wood shops, metal-work, automotive repair, drawing, painting, and sculpture but not ceramics. Ceramics, however, sounded like a good bet. It required all sorts of equipment, and you did not have to be a talented genius to make an ashtray or whatever.

I dug out all the ceramics catalogues from among the many which someone had amassed in the files. They listed package orders, supplies figured out for classes of 20 or 40 students per semester! I selected Western (or California) Type kilns. I had never seen or used one, but they offered the advantage of open-top-loading, which would allow you to stack the kiln vertically and use every inch of space. I also ordered turning wheels, drying cabinets, etc., and turned the whole thing into Procurement on Wednesday. I received the whole thing back on Thursday. Procurement had sought approval from the Corps of Engineers who refused to approve electrical equipment that did not have UL Sanction.

I raced back to my catalogues and substituted AB Dick front-loading kilns and saved the day.

My next big job was to convince the Special Service Officers at the fifteen Army Bases to set up positions for civilian Arts and Crafts Directors, actively recruit qualified people to fill these positions, and get it all synchronized into statistical nirvana.

I worked on the Special Service Officers in accordance with my estimate of their intelligence, stressing morale, the advantage of having a soldier who could fix his own car in an Armored Division, and in extreme cases, the V.D. rate. I found some outstanding Crafts Directors on my own. One, an Art Teacher from deepest Alabama, with 20 years experience during with she had (can you believe this!), worked her salary up from $70 to $90 a month.

One day, a breezy woman in some kind of uniform arrived from Attu, Alaska. Her appearance reminded me of the screen actress, Marie Dressler, who was usually romantically paired with Wallace Beery. Her "Arthuritis," she told me, bothered her in Alaska, where she had been teaching soldiers to carve such things as ivory walrus tusks, etc. Her biggest gripe about the job was officer's wives, who thought that their husband's rank meant that they could walk off and leave her shop in a mess. She soon had convinced them "otherwise"!

Now, this caught my interest. I Immediately thought of the Captain from Special Services at the V.A. Hospital in Hot Springs, Ark. He had been a Sergeant in the Regular Army who had become a Captain in the Reserves, and most of all, he reminded me of Wallace Beery! When I told him of her feud with officer's wives, he was very interested, as I had expected he would be. He hired her by phone as she sat in my office, and they were married eighteen months later.

Fort Polk (nee Camp Polk), in Louisiana, had recently been reactivated (a process connected with recent events in Korea) ; and it had been staffed with personnel deemed excess, useless, unwanted, and otherwise expendable, by the other fourteen Army Bases in the Fourth Army Area. In addition to the many administrative problems that loom up during "activation," the quality of its new personnel who had been thrust together into a fluid and unstable situation, had given Fort Polk an unenviable reputation.

To compound its problems, Hurricane Bertha had swept by the East Texas coast and was supposedly heading for Louisiana.

Thus, when Major Dobbins put down his phone, stretched, spun around in his chair, and said, "Well, we don't have to worry about Hurricane Bertha no more," we were all somewhat relieved.

"Why?" asked someone, "What happened?"

"Well," said the Major, "It's heading for Fort Polk, and they'll sure screw it up."

Shortly thereafter, I was told that Fort Polk's Special Services Officer had hired a civilian Arts and Crafts Director, and I was asked to go there, check him out, and get him off to a good start, in view of the local chaos.

I flew out to Fort Polk with three Colonels, three Majors, and a Captain to take their notes, in the Commanding General's leather-lined plane. It felt like being in a wallet. There was very little vibration and hardly any noise.

The biggest Arts and Crafts program at Fort Polk was Automotive Repair, inasmuch as there was a three to six month waiting list at the tiny service station in the nearest town, Leesville. Everyone was motivated to at least try to repair their own car in the old motor pool shop appropriated by Special Services.

While I was there, the new Director told me of a famous "Rockhound," who lived in Leesville. This old "Lapidary," Willie Smith, was world famous among those who followed the same hobby, buying rocks from him or trading specimens.

We drove over to his home and knocked on his door. An elderly woman looked out and sized us up immediately. "You must be rock people," she said. "He's out back."

In the course of the afternoon, he showed us a huge power saw for slicing rocks, a giant tumbler for polishing them, and a house and garage full of rocks of every kind, piled all over the place. Louisiana was famous for fossilized trees to be found in swamps, as well as agates and other semiprecious stones, and even an occasional diamond. Before our visit was over we had booked him for a series of lectures at Fort Polk and in his shop.

When it was time to return to San Antonio, I was dropped off at the air strip, where I waited for my luxury flight home in the "General's Leather Wallet," but alas, it had departed with all of the Officers on the day that it had arrived.

Then I saw a historical sight, a rusty prop-driven two-seater with a scratched-up plastic top, some sort of WWII or even WWI relic; probably an Observation Plane of some kind.

I said to the soldier at the desk, "Don't tell me that old thing still flies."

"It's your plane," he said. When I gulped, he continued, "But you can take the bus to New Orleans and try to get on a commercial flight."

I thought of all the time that would be wasted when I was so looking forward to getting home.

Resignedly, I carried my valise to the flying relic. The pilot looked to be about twelve years old. He strapped a parachute on me and showed me what to do if I had to abandon the plane in flight. He also told me to keep my feet away from the center of the floor, where the steering mechanism was exposed, and then I climbed into the back seat and he slid the plastic cover over us.

We took off with a roar and a great deal of vibration. Somewhere in the middle of Texas, he tilted the little plane and pointed down to a hanger and air strip. "That's where I just finished my flight course," he yelled. "Great," I said. I did not ask about his grades.

I was grateful when we landed at Kelly Air Force Base in San Antonio. I guess I was too dizzy to bend down and kiss the ground.

I outlasted a few Special Service Officers, one of whom made a major tactical error by granting a newspaper interview. When the paper announced that the Special Services Officer had announced a new Fourth Army Photo and Art Contest, all 5 foot 4 inches of General "Iron Pants" (his legitimate name escapes me), in his khaki shorts, stormed into the Special Services Officer's office and slammed the door shut. This did not prevent anyone in the building from hearing "Iron Pants" chew out our boss. "You do not announce anything," he said over and over. "Only THE COMMANDING GENERAL *announces.* Is that understood?" This went on for ten minutes without variations, and short intervals in which our Light Colonel tearfully apologized over and over.

I know that in my own case, and I am pretty certain that the same is true of anyone who worked at Fort Sam Special Services that day, we are probably all a little reluctant to say anything to a member of the Fourth Estate, as well as to attorneys, doctors, hospital personnel, or undertakers.

In the midst of all this excitement, I took a few days off to attend *a* meeting of the College Art Association in Cleveland. I had sent my dissertation on "Saint Sebastian in Art" to my latest Advisor, Professor Millard Miess, a specialist in the Early Renaissance. I had heard nothing from him for a year and a half. I wrote to him knowing that he was scheduled to read a paper at one of the meetings, and I suggested that he could bring my Dissertation along and save the bother of mailing it.

When he arrived, he handed me the Dissertation and his only comment was that it had too many commas. From what I could see of his pencilled corrections, he had flipped through the first eight pages during his flight to Cleveland, and otherwise not even glanced at it for a year and a half.

I sat down in one of the hallways, boiling inside, right next to Professor Ken Lindsay from Harpur College, which then was still in Endicott, N.Y. He saw my name plate and remembered my name from the application I had made for a job at Harpur about eight years earlier. He asked me if I was still interested. I told him that I was, and in talking to him, I realized that even if I had persisted in my earlier application, they would still have selected Lindsay, who at that time had already completed his Doctorate at Wisconsin University.

About a month later, I flew into Binghamton to be interviewed for the opening at Harpur College. I found out later, that after meeting me, President Glenn Bartle had called the Art Department at Columbia University to find out if I was close to earning my Doctorate. He spoke to the new Chairman, Rudolph Wittkower, who told him that his Department owed me an apology for their cavalier and sloppy handling of my case. He assured President Bartle that I would be invited to defend my Dissertation within two weeks, and that I would absolutely receive my Doctorate before the term began at Harpur College in September.

That was fine, but no one thought about telling me, and as I flew North for the third time, I was getting so angry that I was probably talking to myself. It had been eleven years since I started at Columbia where I broke all records for completing the requirements (course work, comprehensives in architecture, painting, and sculpture, and three language tests), everything except the approval of my Dissertation.

I arrived about a half hour early and sat on the steps outside the building, thinking of all those wasted years.

Finally I went in to defend the Dissertation. I had a distinguished panel including two historians. I must still be angry, because I am unable to recall their names, so let's say Fledermaus and Hasenpfeffer, and fortunately no Meyer Schapiro. He was in Europe that summer, I believe. Prof. James McPharlin Davis, my most recent Advisor, chaired the panel, signaling it to begin.

Herr Professor Fledermaus had two pages of questions, single-spaced. This is an *oral examination,* I told myself. I waited until he had read all of his questions, not listening to any of them.

"Are there any other questions?" I asked.

Herr Professor Hasenpfeffer, smiling to show his good will, said, "You have a very exciting discovery placed in the Appendix of your book, which would have made a fine Dissertation all by itself. I refer to your account of a series of manuscripts painted at a time when the monasteries were struggling to keep their independence in the face of royal efforts to control them. You showed how this struggle was reflected in a group of manuscript paintings which isolated the royal witnesses from portrayals of the *Madonna,* or the *Crucifixion,* and even the *Martyrdom of Saint Sebastian.* The Kings and their courtiers are on the left (or *Sinister),* page, with the Holy figures on the right page; and of course, the interesting one is Saint Sebastian who appears on the upper right hand corner of a page, while the Emperor and his archers are found on the lower left hand corner of the same page. I just wondered why this exciting and interesting information was almost hidden in the Appendix."

My reply was, that it was the judgment of Rennselaer Lee, my earliest advisor, that this material was too controversial and therefore belonged in the Appendix. I concluded by adding, "Your Advisor contributes the benefit of his experience, and if you ignore his advice then what function does he serve?"

There were no other questions, and I was asked to wait outside.

After five minutes of numbness, Professor Davis came out, holding up his hands defensively. "It's all right! It's all right! There are just a few typos that have to be corrected and you are done."

I took a deep breath.

"You seemed to be very angry," he said.

"Well dammit!" I said. "Wouldn't you be?"

I thought about getting the typos corrected in San Antonio for about two minutes. Then I looked into the Yellow Pages for a typing service. When I got there they divided the pages needing corrections among four typists and told me to come back in an hour. I did, and replaced the corrected pages, and filed all the copies but mine at the Columbia Art History Department.

Imagine my shock about seven years later when I received a letter from Mary Chamberlain, the Art Librarian, saying that page 82 was missing, and that a student from NYU, one Robert Baron, needed it. Luckily I had my own copy to xerox and mail in.

The funny thing was that Robert Baron was one of my ex-students at the State University in Binghamton, whom I had advised on his Master's Thesis. He had then gone to the New York University Fine Arts Institute to work on a Doctorate, and selected the subject of Saint Irene, who had nursed Saint Sebastian's arrow wounds. His NYU Advisor had directed him to Columbia's Art Library, saying that he could not do justice to a Saint Sebastian theme without consulting the Zupnick Dissertation on file there.

Anyway, before heading North again, I had one more job to do for Fourth Army.

It was, believe it or not, to create a Fourth Army Model Airplane Team to compete in the All Army Model Airplane Contest at Fort Lewis in the State of Washington. Elimination Contests were "conducted" (Army lingo) , at all of my fifteen Bases, and the Fourth Army Finals were at Fort Sill, Oklahoma. I was never a model airplane enthusiast, by the way; I had made one when I was a boy, and watched it destroy itself on its first flight of two minutes.

Anyway, I was the Teams manager as we left for Fort Lewis in the great State of Washington.

I had never traveled with a team before. I felt a little bit like a momma duck herding my ducklings at various airports. We had dropped this young Lieutenant off to visit his wife who had just given him a son, and he caught up with us at Fort Lewis.

The contest began, and one event immediately caught my attention: Aerial Combat. In it, two opponents took off, each bearing a colored paper tail. The modeler who cut off his opponent's tail first was the winner; however, both planes flew until they ran out off gas. In each combat, the men from my Fourth Army Team almost immediately cut off their opponent's tail, but then their opponent contrived to get both controlling wires entangled, and made both planes crash. A pyrrhic victory!

Then I found out why they were so profligate, and that truly upset me. The Eighth Army Headquarters, our host, had called Washington, D.C. to find out how many planes their team was allowed to have on hand for Aerial Combat. "As many as you want," they were told. Then the Colonel in charge of the All Army Contest thought that this information should be passed on to Third Army, whose Headquarters were in the same building in Washington, D.C.; but they had told no one else! And my great team had come with one plane per man, according to the usual protocol for such contests, only to have them destroyed on the first day, after they had won every contest!

Well, I was up all night with my entire team, building combat planes to meet the challenges they would have to face on the next day. This put me into a really good mood, and when I ran into the stupid Colonel from Washington, D.C., I got him up against a wall and chewed him out as if I were "General Iron Pants." I had already given my notice at Fourth Army Headquarters so I outranked him. I was a civilian.

After all, *My Team* was best in almost every category, including hand-launched gliders. There was this Sergeant on my team who had redesigned the glider with incredibly-articulated wings that caught breezes from every angle and kept his glider flying, it seemed, forever. And there was the young Lieutenant who had dropped off in Arizona to see his wife and their new baby. He flew B-planes, a tiny and noisy craft that seemed to be all engine, and took first place easily.

When I got back to Fort Sam, I found that the stupid Colonel had beaten me back with a tel-ex message. I guess he was afraid of what I might say about his running of the contest, because his message said that I showed outstanding team spirit and devotion to the men on my team.

My gypsy family, now four-strong, sold our house, got rid of most of the furnishings, mailed what we could to my new office, and took off in our battered five-year old Chevy, heading North.

We stopped at my in-laws in Brooklyn to leave our two little girls with them temporarily, and drove to the Triple Cities to look for a new home. We found our house in one day with the help of my new Chairman, Ken Lindsay, who had helped the owner with some of its construction. It was a pre-fab, a Tech-Built, the smallest of three in the area; and with the equity from our house in San Antonio, and whatever cash we had, we managed to take over the reasonable G.I. Mortgage.

Not long after, Toby said, "Let's have one more for the road," and our son, Matthew was born in Wilson Hospital in Johnson City, across the Susquehanna.

I promise not to bore you with all of the usual back-biting and politicking that goes on in The Groves of Academe. It is too distressingly scabrous and scrofulous (technical terms) to go into, and I tried, successfully, I think, to remain uncontaminated by its stench from 1958 until my retirement in 1985.

I can say, with appealing modesty, that I was quite good at my trade, with about *45* publications, plus seminars and public lectures here and abroad. For example, I was an invited participant at the 400th Anniversary of Erasmus in Belgium, at a Seminar on Plato and Aristotle in the Renaissance at the University of Tours in France, and I was invited to read a paper on Bruegel in Yugoslavia at the International Meeting of Art Historians, and I had other invitations to Columbia University and Oswego College.

As an artist in several mediums, I also exhibited in one-man and group shows in Michigan, Illinois, the Southwest, several times in upstate New York, and once in the U.S.S.R. I never painted myself into a corner, doctrinally or otherwise, not once; and I was far from adverse to communicating ideas to those who were looking for them.

Chapter X
MY TWO RENAULTS

Toby and I became addicted to Europe, going there at least eight times for a few weeks each time during the summers, ostensibly for art-historical research, usually with grants to pay for some of it. In order to minimize the complexities of travelling through the spaces between Museums and Cathedrals, we used rented cars, which were often part of the air fare package. Often the cars contributed to our adventures.

For instance, I remember once in Florence, Italy, when I asked for directions at a gas station, that the proprietor stopped traffic and sent us the wrong way around a traffic circle and I drove with my eyes shut.

Or the time when a patriotic French Mobil Gas Station attendant put gasoline into the oil tank of our Volkswagen which put the car out of commission in Longjumeau, about 15 miles from our hotel in Paris.

In Madrid's Airport I stood behind a huge Texan at the car rental counter, who was returning a car after fifteen minutes. When this was pointed out by the woman at the counter, he said "They ain't no-ways I am gonna drive out there."

I accidentally dropped my keys into the trunk of a fiat in Padua, and the rental agent sent over a car thief (I swear!), who jimmied it open. But it was even more interesting in Madrid when we parked our rented Renault next to an outdoor Police formation and its door automatically locked, with its key tantalizingly sparkling in the starter.

Two of the cops, looking seven feet tall in their bull-fighterish helmets saw what had happened and they whistled for a scrawny little guy with long arms, who ran across the street to join us. The two cops put all of their weight on the slightly-opened window and opened it a bit more. The scrawny guy reached in and opened the door lock. As he ran away, one of the cops yelled in Spanish, "Don't let me catch you," and the other one told me that the little guy was "the best car thief in Madrid."

Toby and I were driving through the Basque area in Southern France when we noticed an interesting Romanesque church in the little town of Robuillac. It was a medley of tenth and eleventh century styles looking as if it had been assembled over at least two hundred years, and reflecting either local changes of taste or perhaps the influence of different artists and craftsmen who had passed through the area in search of work.

We stopped at a combined post office and grocery store, hoping to get some bread and cheese for lunch and postcards to send home to the children. Out of curiosity I asked the young man, the postal-grocery clerk if he had any idea about when the church had been built.

"I don't know," he said. He spun around in his chair and spoke to a very old woman seated behind him, knitting booties for some lucky child.

"Grandma," he said, "Do you know how old the church is?"

She put the knitting down on her lap and smoothed it out. "I don't know," she replied, "But it is older than I am."

But our best car experiences were to come when the State University of New York actually paid me (would you believe it?) to go to Fontainebleau about 40 miles from Paris, to act as liaison and godfather for whatever music and art students from its various branches wanted to take advantage of studying with faculty provided by the Ecole Des Beaux-Arts of Paris and Fontainebleau's world-famous music program.

I was very happy to spend time at Fontainebleau, which I had been unable to visit when the patriotic garage attendant put gasoline in my Volkswagen's oil tank. Fontainebleau was important in my area of study, because in the Sixteenth Century, King Francois I, who was so enamored with the Florentine Neo-Platonically inspired Manneristic Style, that he had had his summer Palace in Fontainebleau decorated with frescoes by Il Rosso Fiorentino and Primaticcio. This was in contrast with his contemporaries of equal rank. Henry VIII of England, preferred the matter-of-fact German, Hans Holbein, while Charles V, the hyper-religious Holy Roman Emperor, who tried to turn his Court at the Escorial into a "Second Rome," preferred the sensually fleshy nudes of the Venetian painter, Titian. There is in fact, a letter from Charles V to Titian, which tells the artist that the Emperor is so delighted with the frontal view of the model who posed for Titian's Venus, that he would like the artist to paint another picture of her showing her backside. Perhaps this explains the unusual pose of Venus in the "Venus and Adonis" in the Prado Museum.

But to get back to the Fontainebleau summers. It seemed absurd to rent cars for a few months when the only distinguishing feature of our cars at home was their age; so we purchased Renaults in each of the two summers, cars that found it agreeable to meet us at Orly Airport, and then to follow us home on cargo ships.

On the second summer, my wife Toby and I decided to bring our three children along so that they could have the wonderful experience of seeing France and studying alongside college students. Also, for the first time we would not be missing our children and worrying about them for the whole summer. Anne, the oldest and the one in our family with the most dependable memory, tells me she was eighteen, Julia sixteen and a half, and Matthew ten and a half.

The previous Summer we had purchased a Renault-10, which, after its arrival in the States, proved itself to be too small for both a family car and a luggage transport, so we sprang for a red Renault- 16, a French version of the American station-wagon.

We had rented a villa in the town of Fontainebleau complete with a Jardiniere who always smelled of herring and wine, at considerably less than the hotel's rates, from the owner, Madame Philardeau, a doctor's widow who preferred to spend her summers with her daughter in Nice.

Our Renault- 16 would stall every morning at the first corner stop sign. I brought it to the Renault Factory, but either my French was so poor (quite possibly), or their mechanics so bad (quite possibly) that they could not fix it. Actually the problem was solved two years later by a Florida "Cracker" in a roadside gas station, who had "never seen no Reenot of any number," who figured out that all the transmission needed was "a little old lock-washer to hold it all together."

Anyway, it was a great summer. My wife and the kids attended the art classes at Fontainebleau Palace. Toby told me that she felt so sorry for the nude models, who turned blue in the unheated studio; and I thought that this perhaps might be a clue to Picasso's "Blue Period;" and maybe a good subject for a quick article for the College Art Journal.

My son, Matt, became a local celebrity. Acting on his own, he crumpled some chicken-wire fencing into an armature about as tall as he was. Then he molded burlap, soaked in plaster of paris around it and painted the resultant figure with clothing and red hair. The red-headed French Art Instructor gleefully pointed to it as his portrait and I enjoyed overhearing a conversation in which some music people lauded a 12-year-old prodigy, and the art people countered with the example of Matt, who, they bragged, wasn't even eleven.

Anyway, Toby and I were in the Renault going through the Town of Nemours on the way to Paris, when we finally located La Musee, identified by a tiny sign, about 1 x 6 inches, affixed to a marvelous wrought-iron fence. All during our first Summer and part of the second I had been asking myself why I thought that the name of the town had some historical significance, and then I remembered that Rabelais in his book, "Gargantua and Pantegruel," the very same book that got me the job as Messenger at First Army Headquarters, if you recall, continually made up jokes about his Patron, the Duc de Nemours. I thought, if there was a Duke, there must have been a Palace, and if there had been a Palace, whatever was left of it had to be a Museum.

A musee was mentioned in the Michelin Guide, which did not even devote a map to a town as small as Nemours, and no one in town that I spoke to had any idea of where such a Museum might be located.

So that when I saw this tiny sign out of the corner of my eye, I almost caused a chain accident. I parked down the street and Toby and I walked back to the sign. It was fastened to a magnificent wrought-iron fence that enclosed a granite-floored patio that led to marble steps which mounted to two huge oak-framed glass doors beside another copy of the diminutive "La Musee" sign.

We ran up the steps. I rang the bell button above the little sign. No one answered. I shook the doors. Nothing. Suddenly a wooden shutter in the courtyard at a window a story above our heads rattled open, and a burly woman leaned out with her fists on the window-sill.

"What do you want?" she bellowed in French.

"I would like to see the Museum," I replied.

"It is not possible," she said" It is closed."

"Oh," I said. "Well, when will it be open?"

"Never," was her answer.

"Never?" was all I could think of saying.

As an explanation, she said, "Monsieur Le Director is dead." I realized the likelihood that, as it was the common practice in provincial museums in Europe to install families as caretakers, she was probably the Director's widow. "I am very sorry to hear that," I said, "But I suppose that after a reasonable time the museum will reopen?"

"No," she replied, looking a little flustered. "When we buried him, he had the key in his pocket." Toby and I sat down on the steps and laughed, and the woman violently slammed the shutters back in place.

The school at Fontainebleau had a ten-day break associated with Bastille Day. Toby and I had watched the parade the previous year, with the Eiffel Tower as background, and we swore that the entire French Army and Air Force had participated. Newspapers all across Europe expressed alarm at this demonstration of French military potency, describing it as "threatening" and with charming anachronistic understatement as "sabre rattling." Rather than see more of the same, we booked a hotel in London, finding its advertisement in the English-language *Tribune*.

We drove to Le Havre to get the ferry to Dover. I was waiting at the right turn into the road to the ferry as a stream of cars came out of it., when all of my children pointed out that I was allowed to make the turn because all of the British cars were driving on the wrong side of the road.

Driving down the highway towards London, I asked Toby from time to time if I could pass a truck. "Why are you asking me?" she asked. "Because I am on the right side of our car, and I can't see," I told her.

Just before London I came to a traffic circle, and after circling it twice I stopped to ask directions of some men who were working on the road.

One of them said, "You go round about the round-about, and take A1." I was going to ask him to repeat it, but I slowly began to comprehend his meaning. At the tiny hotel our three children were given a room two flights above us. "Is there an elevator?" I asked. The lady who managed the hotel said. "This is not the Ritz, but we do give a good breakfast." Both statements were true.

"This is great," Anne said. "They talk English." Julie said, "Sort of." "Kind of," said Matt. We had an interesting time, and we stopped at Westminster on the return trip. When we landed in France, Toby said, "After you got used to driving on the wrong side of the road, I think it would be best for me to drive here. "She was right as usual.

Anyway, after many other adventures in France and at home, the red Renault-16 abandoned us before we could enter the Oakdale Mall in Johnson City. It died of a broken crankshaft (whatever that is), worn out no doubt from not stalling at the first corner every morning. It turned out to be too complicated to order a new crankshaft or to find one in a junkyard so we advertised that we had a Renault-16 with a broken crankshaft and a mailman from Deposit, NY bought it. He owned three other Renault-16s which he cannibalized to keep one running, because he said it was the best car for delivering mail on snowy days.

But I really wanted to tell you about the Renault-10 that we had purchased a year earlier. It was a sort of off-white or off-gray, a French color as off as French-bronze (whatever that is), is to real bronze. It was a kind of cute car. Its engine was in the back, so you put luggage or shopping under the hood in front. There was also a mysterious little black box that the manual said was an electronic automatic transmission. I was always a little afraid of it.

Anyway, I shipped it to the States as I was to do a year later with the red Renault 16, and a few weeks after it arrived I received a computer printout from the great city of New York announcing that a gray-white Renault 10, with French License plate 20002NL, registered in my name, had been illegally parked in front of Columbia Presbyterian Hospital on such and such hours on such and such a day; and that as a result I owed the great city of what is it, 14,000,000 people, a fine of *$50.*

Fortunately, because I hate to clutter myself with paper unsuitable to write or draw on, I still had a printout of the shipper's invoice which seemed to me to prove that during the hours when the "crime" was committed, the said Renault-10 of whatever color was somewhere between Le Havre in France and Elizabeth in New Jersey. I sent this bit of paper in lieu of the fine and asked them to explain how such an error was possible in this era of high-tech miracles. No answer was given.

Now, the Renault-10 was a car with a real personality. I refer to her as if she was feminine, because she tolerated us to a point, even when we contradicted her own drummer. On cold mornings, when I backed her out of the garage, she would whimper piteously, and more than once on an icy Route 26, her rear engine would spin us completely around as if she was trying to head back to the warm garage.

She was very French in that she would only accept high test gasoline, preferably estate-bottled in a good year. But for all of her willfulness, the R-10 gave excellent mileage, which is why I don't understand one thing. I brought her back from Elizabeth, New Jersey on less than half a tank of gas. During the week she accompanied me to work, and I filled her tank every Friday on the way home. I then turned her over to my two daughters for the weekend and was surprised each Monday to find the tank to be nearly empty. I still have no explanation. Perhaps she would go off on her own, trying to find a boat headed for Le Havre.

Oh yes. It turned out that the R-10 had a romantic streak. She brought my daughter, Julie, together with her future husband, Gary, when Julie traded her in for a less-opinionated car on his car lot.

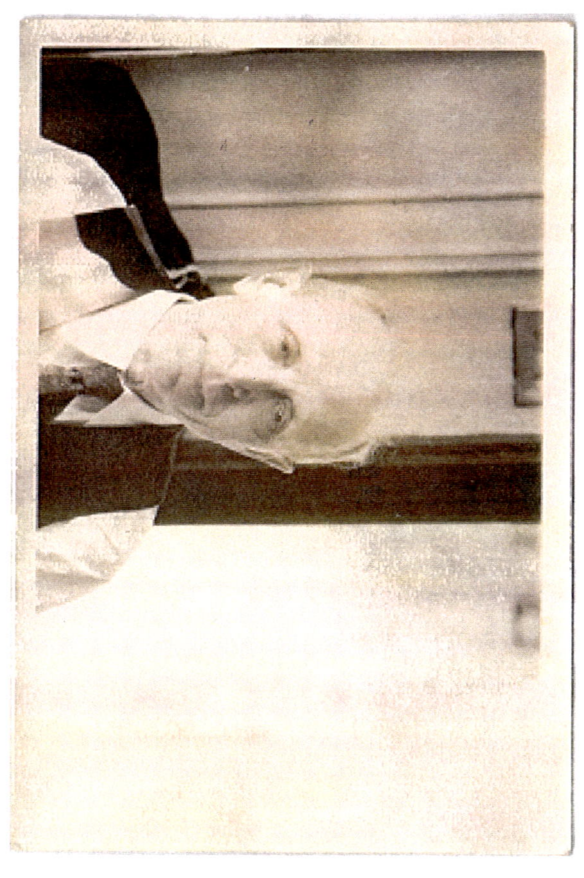

Irv's Grandpa, Harris Goldfein

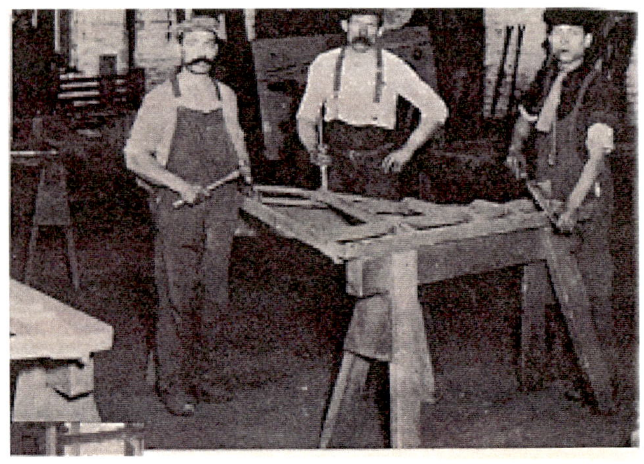

Harris Goldfein on the Left
working at Steinwary Piano Plant in 1908

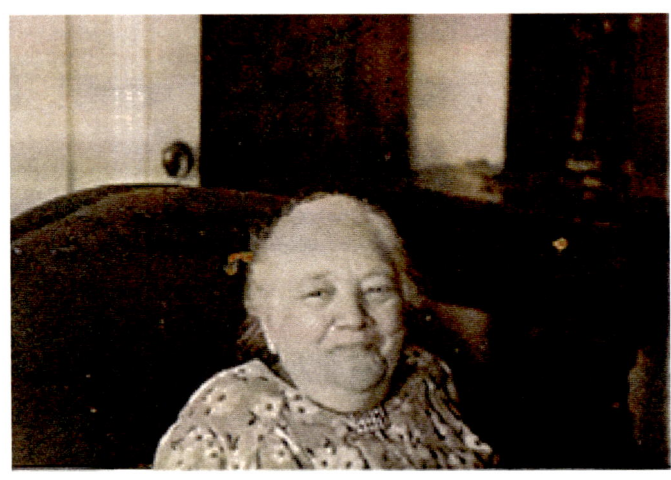

Irv's Grandma, Jenny Goldfein

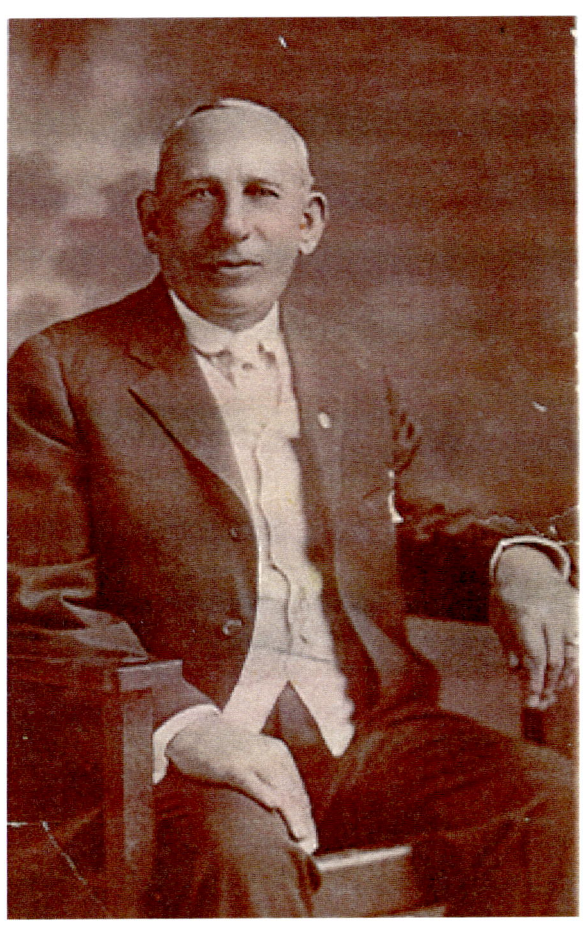

Irv's Grandpa, Col. Abraham Zupnick

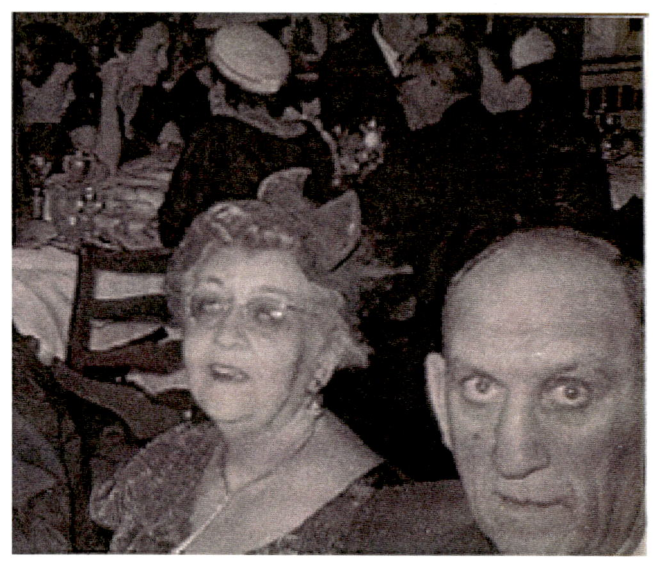

Irv's Mom, Kate, and Step-father, Ruben Katz

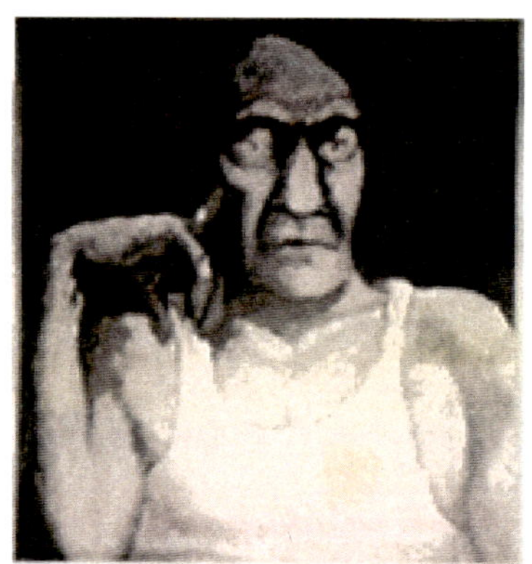

Irv's Portrait of Ruben Katz
in the Centennial Show at CCNY (1957)

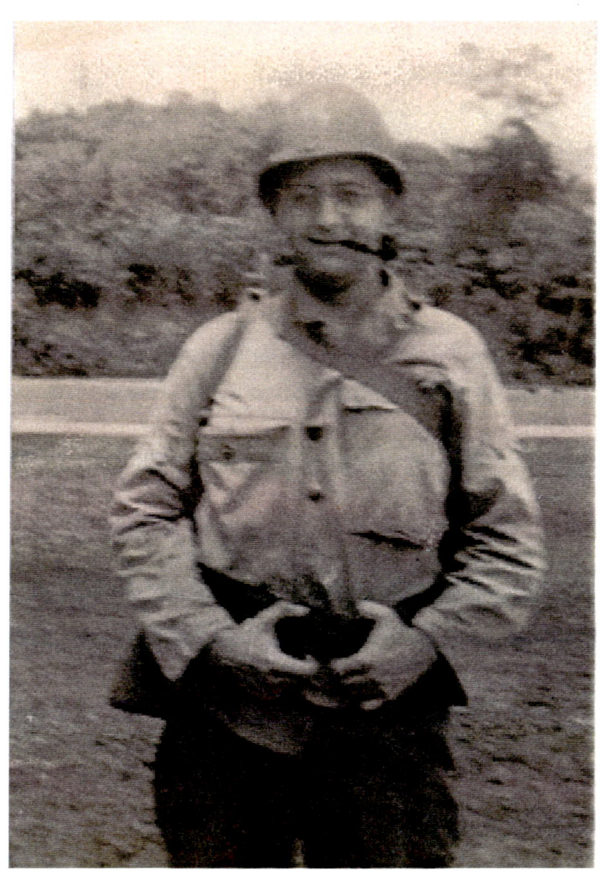

Sgt. Irving Zupnick at Fort Clayton,
Panama Canal Zone (1945)

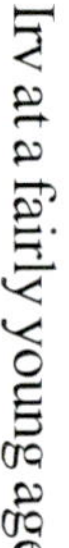

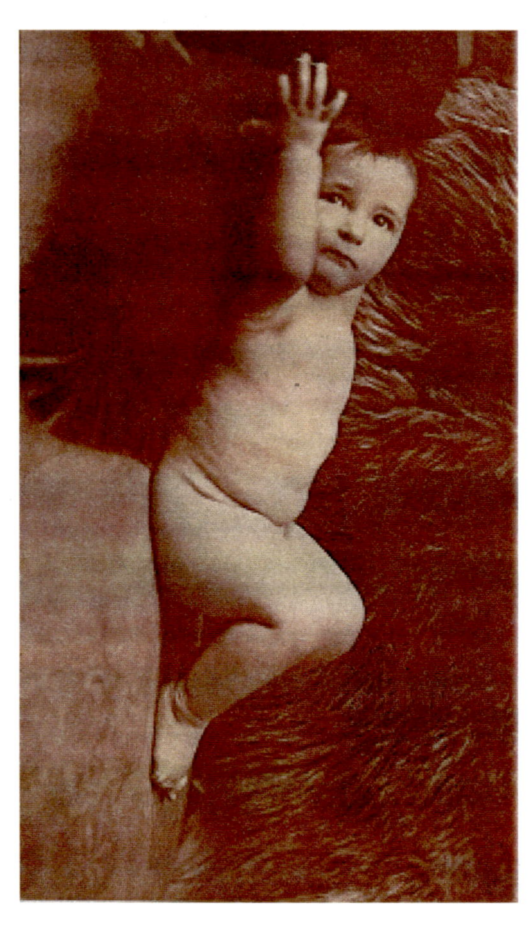

Irv at a fairly young age

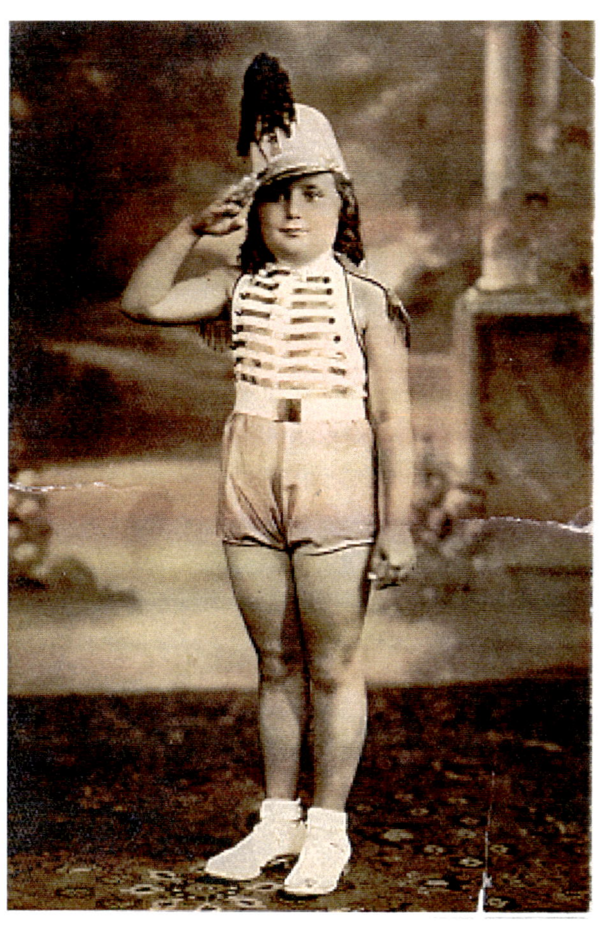

Toby at a wonderful stage

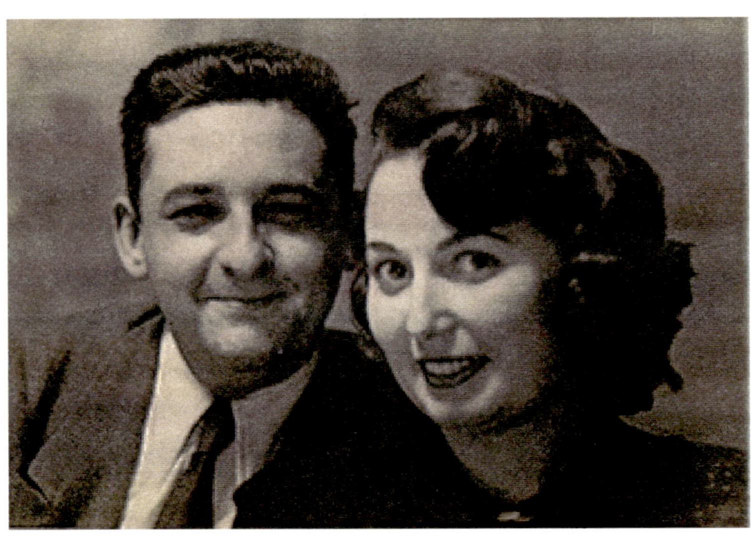

Toby and Irving, Engaged, April 1949

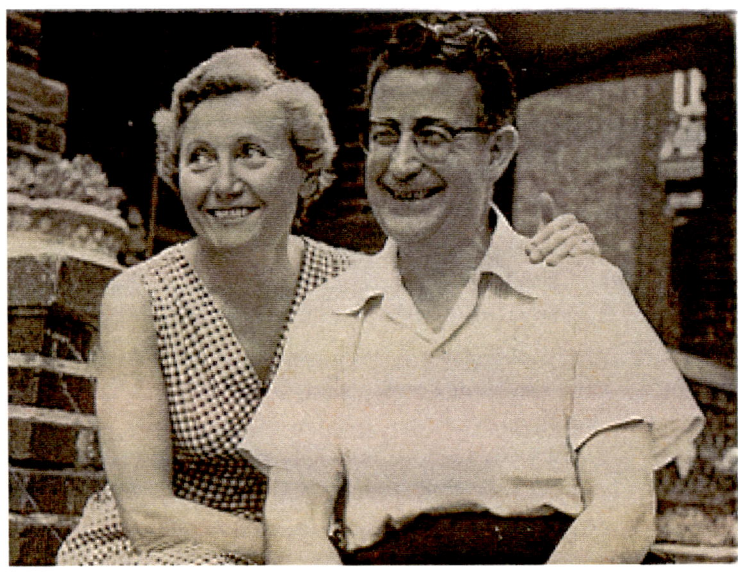

Bertha and David Wiesen, Toby's parents

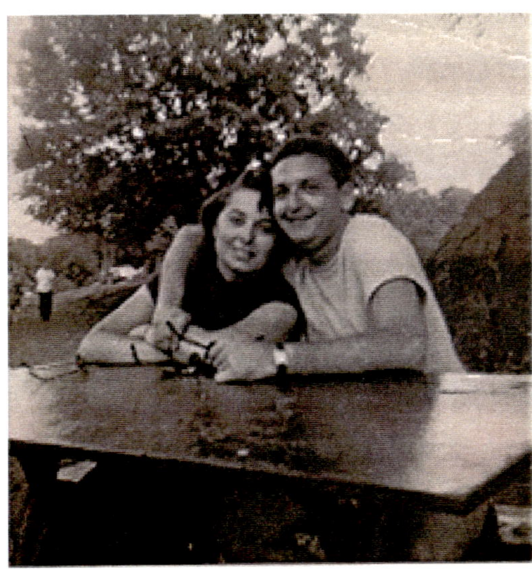

Toby and Irving (1950)

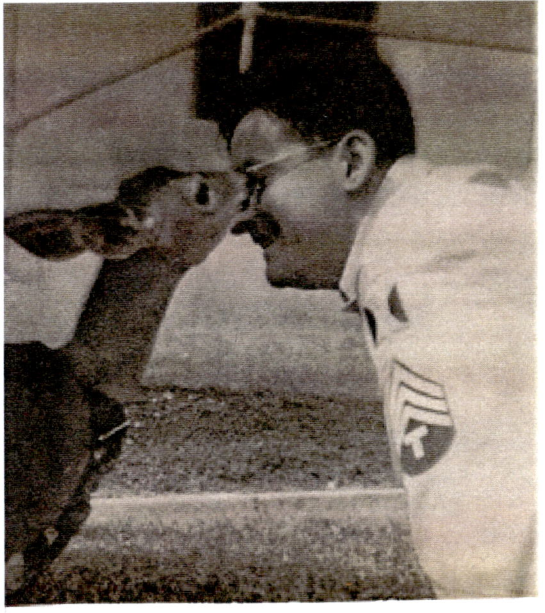

Irv with a very deer friend in Panama

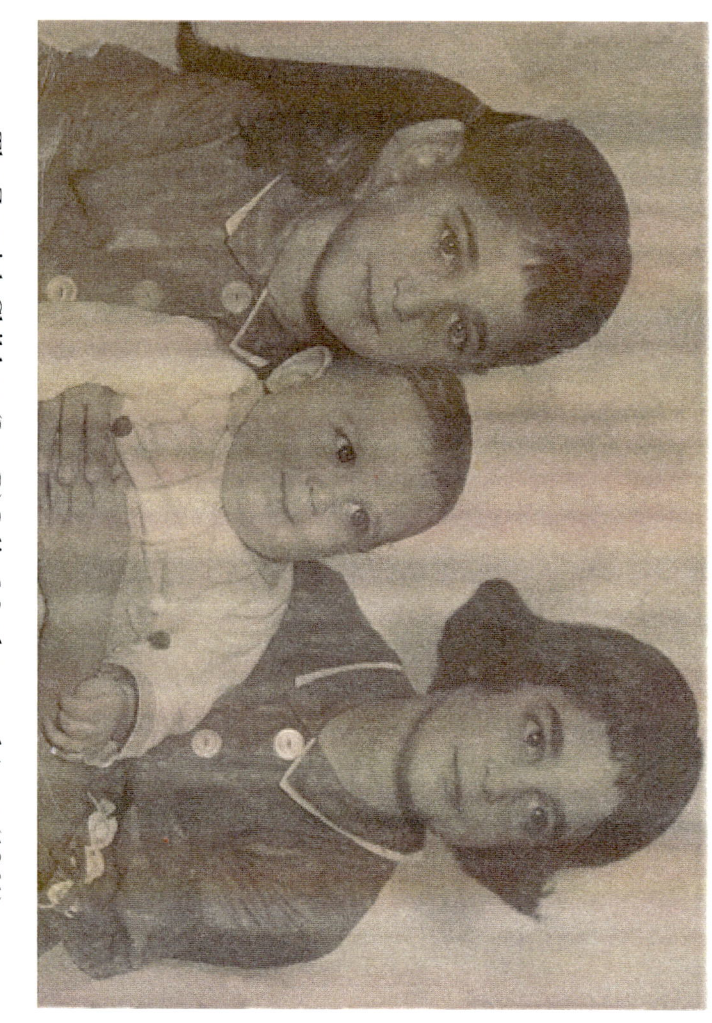

The Zupnick Children (L to R) Julia, Matthew, and Anne (1961)

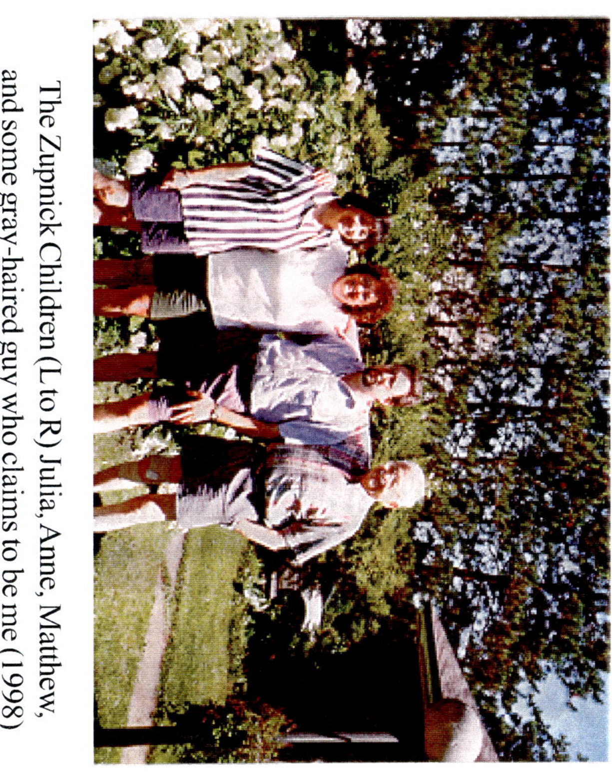

The Zupnick Children (L to R) Julia, Anne, Matthew, and some gray-haired guy who claims to be me (1998)

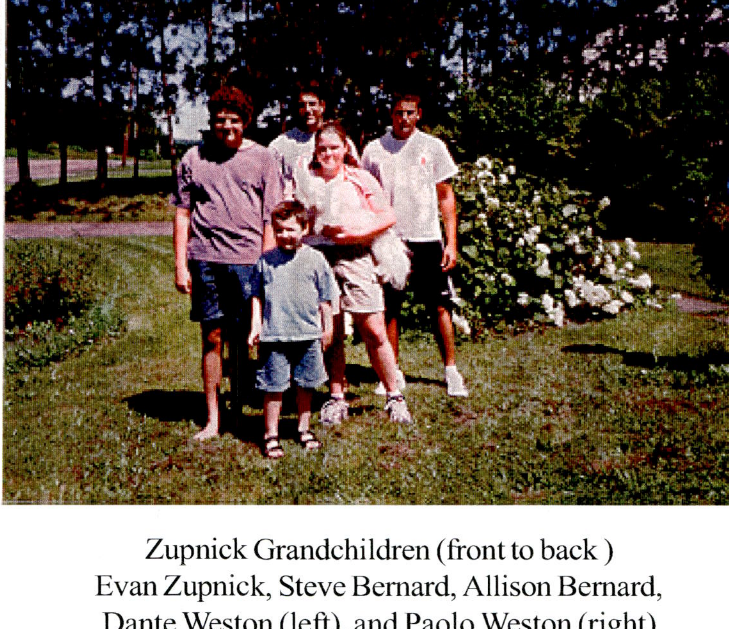

Zupnick Grandchildren (front to back)
Evan Zupnick, Steve Bernard, Allison Bernard,
Dante Weston (left), and Paolo Weston (right)

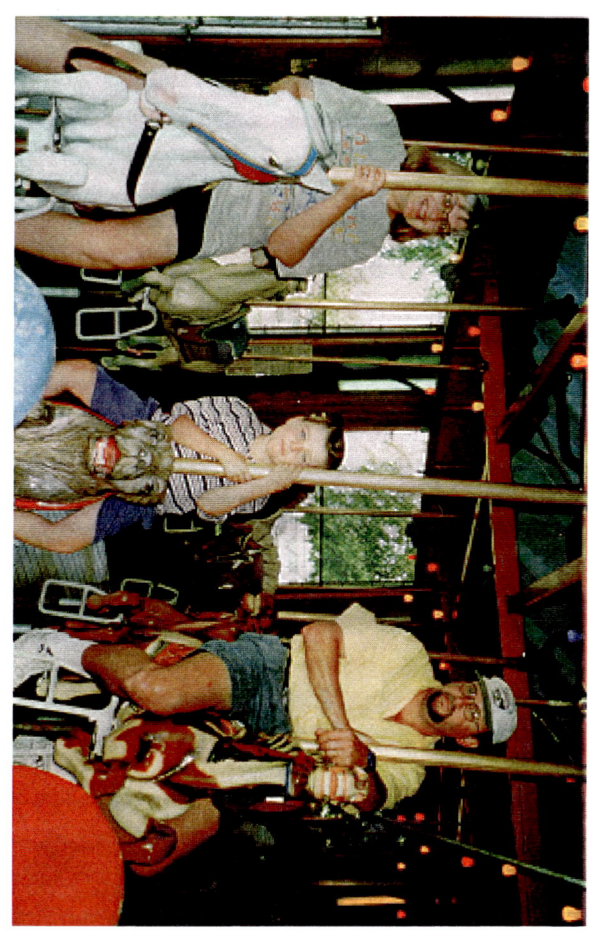

Stefanie, Mrs. Matt Zupnick, Evan, and Matt

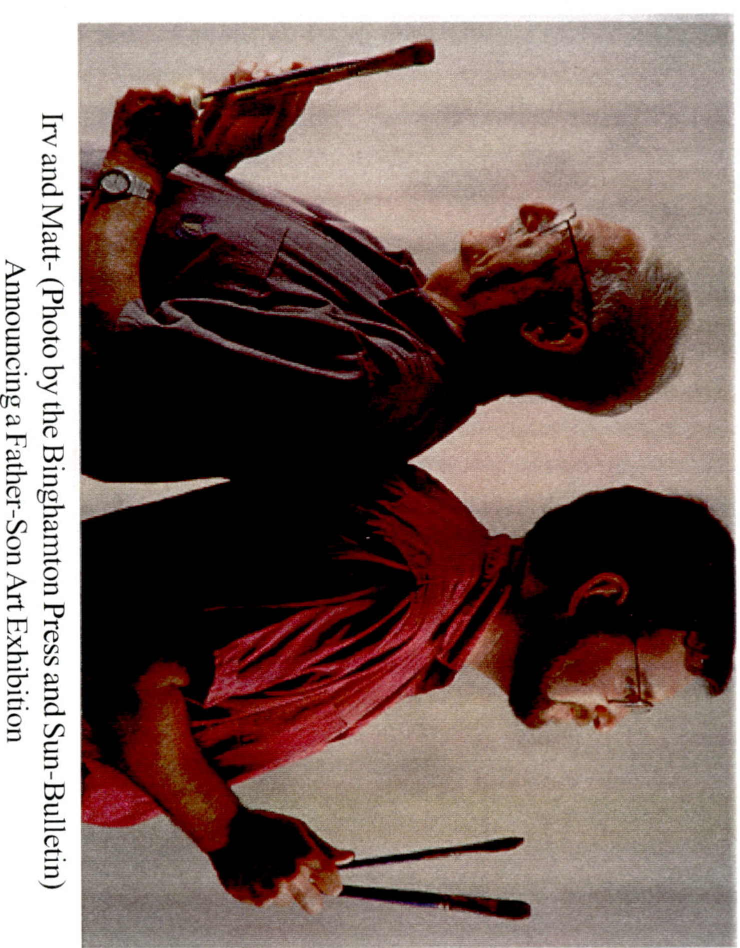

Irv and Matt- (Photo by the Binghamton Press and Sun-Bulletin) Announcing a Father-Son Art Exhibition

Chapter XI
THE RIGHT TO LIFE

Although I guess I should not be, I have to admit to being amused when I read about the casualties (hunters shot by other hunters or by themselves), on the first days of the deer-hunting season. I even wrote a letter which they published in Binghamton's *Press & Sun-Bulletin* a couple of years ago. I cannot find a copy of it, but it went something like this:

> Don't let their soft brown eyes fool you. You've seen the headlines! "Six Hunters Wounded On The First Day of The Hunting Season." "Second Day's Hunting Casualties: Four," etc. The deer have had enough, and now they are armed and dangerous! Farmer Jeff Brown swears that he saw a stag, driving a Jeep with a hunter tied across its hood. He is the same farmer, you will remember, who reported last year that a Flying Saucer landed in his corn field and popped half an acre! So, hunters beware! It's a jungle out there!

I became a softy for animals (almost but not quite as much as for children), when I was about 8 or 9, and my dad took me to see the Bronx park Zoo. He bought me a bag of peanuts and they were half gone when I made friends with a squirrel that was so tame he took peanuts right out of my hand. I ran out of them too soon, and I held my index finger between my thumb and the next finger. The squirrel came over and tugged at my index finger gently. Then he backed up, and I swear that he grinned at me. He tried again, backed up and grinned again, and then scampered away. I'll be darned if he didn't get the joke and share it with me!

About two years later, I went to the Morrisania Branch Library in the Bronx, with my mother, and I found an injured sparrow, in a snow-bank. One of its wings was twisted and extended at an awkward angle. I fixed it as well as I could, wrapped it in my scarf, and took it home after we were through with the library. My mom did not say a word, which was remarkable. Usually she would have said, "The bird is probably diseased; don't touch it."

When we returned from the library, I made a splint for the sparrow's wing with a pencil and a shoelace. I kept the bird in a shoebox in my room and fed it with bread crumbs soaked in milk. After a week I removed the splint, and the little fellow began to hop around my room. Within a few hours he began to fly from one piece of furniture to another.

Then my mom spoke for the first time. "You're going to have to turn him loose now that he's well." I agreed and put him on our fire-escape with his shoebox and food. A short while later I looked out and he was gone.

But the wonderful thing was that for a week and a half I would see him flying in circles above our back yard, and I would put his food on our fire-escape, and he would land and eat some. Then, one day he stopped returning and my mom said that probably he had returned to his family, and I said, "I hope so," and tried not to think of any other explanation.

When I was quite young, we had a cat named "Murphy," who would do a sort of dance to the music from our wind-up victorola. He was particularly fond of Chopin. The only problem with Murphy was that when I tried to get him out from under our couch, he would tear my hands to ribbons.

I have had three dogs in my time. Two of them came from my Aunt Frances who bought them for her own children, and found that they were totally uninterested in taking care of them. Since she, herself, was not fond of dogs, I would end up with them. Buddy was the first. Frances brought him to me on the summer that my dad died.

My mom and I had just moved into my grandparents' apartment on the Grand Concourse in the Bronx. I shared a room with my uncle Abe, and my mother shared her sister Rose's room. During the summer Buddy and I were inseparable. As a result, he drove everyone crazy when school started, crying all day until I returned home at 4 P.M.

My mom pointed out that it was not fair either to Buddy or my grandparents to have him crying for so many hours, and that I would have to give him to someone who could take care of him. One day we brought him to my friends, Felix and Johnnie Mujica, who lived miles away.

Years later, maybe five or six, my mother asked me to meet her at the Mujica's apartment so that we all could go shopping together. The boys' Mother and mine were always good friends; and years later I often ran into Jenny Mujica at Columbia University after she had finished cleaning classrooms and offices, and she would give me the latest news about her sons.

Anyway, when I rang the Mujicas' bell, there was a lot of barking. One of the boys opened the door. Holy smoke; there was Buddy. I had forgotten about him over the years. He barked a few more times. Tilted his head to one side, and then he went crazy. He became a white blur, jumping up and down and running around in circles until I picked him up. He licked me all over my face. The guys told me that he had not been so lively for more than two years. I felt pretty low. I had forgotten all about him, but he remembered me.

The second dog that I got from my aunt Frances, when my mother and I had moved to our own apartment, was a frantic fox terrier named Rex, who would run so fast that he was unable to turn without tumbling all over himself. That's about all I remember about that nut!

My third dog, Thunder, whom we got for our children who picked him out of a litter at someone's house, was a tweedy blue and black mixture of Kerry Blue and Scotch Terrier. My children named him Thunder because it was thundering on the afternoon that we brought him home. They picked him because he was the biggest of his litter and a real chow hound who chased his brothers and sisters away from their food.

From the day that we got him we could see that he had a mind of his own. I remember that even as a puppy he would want to go in a different direction than we were heading, and it was either drag him with the leash or carry him. Other than that, Thunder was an honorary child on our street. He played with all of the children as if he were one of them.

One day, everything changed. When I called him for dinner, he spun around and took off down our hill. I found out from people who had seen him, that he led a pack of dogs; that he would turn over garbage cans and they would all join in for dinner. He had become a gourmet preferring je ne sais quoi pot-luck to our dog food.

That we could live with. But he would come back some time during the night or early morning and stretch out at our front door. At 6 A.M., when one of the neighbors got in his car to go to work, Thunder would begin barking for some reason, and I would have to go down and let him in. The mornings were cold, I guess. So he would be glad to come in for a snooze.

But then his life became complicated. Vestal passed a leash law, probably against dogs that knocked over garbage cans. And we had to confine him at the end of a chain close to our garage. He wore his misery like a palpable dark cloud.

We all felt sorry for him, and one day, when I picked him up at the kennel after a trip into New York City, I mentioned that he was a good dog that should be living in a place without a leash law.

Next day someone called about Thunder. Their family was about to move to a farm in New Jersey. They had an old dog and wanted another dog to keep her company. This farm had a couple of acres fenced in, and Thunder would be totally unconfined. "Did I want references?" they asked. "No," I said, "Come and get him."

They did, taking him about twenty miles to Upper Front Street on the other side of Binghamton where they were residing until they left for New Jersey in another two days. Know what? At 6 a.m. next morning there the dog was barking outside my front door at neighbors who were leaving for work. His new owners called us frantically at 8 A.M. to report that he had run off! "He's here," I told them. "Come and get him." They came and left next morning for New Jersey. He has not returned since.

When I was stationed at Fort Clayton in Panama, one of the Post Commanders learned that the Jungle Platoon, an outfit that periodically swept through the local jungles and which was quartered in the barracks next to us, often brought back various animals and birds. They ordered the construction of a zoo for the smaller animals. The "Zoo" was a construction made of pipes and cyclone-fencing, and looked like a transparent airport locker about 30 by 15 feet, and 10 feet high.

It was next to our barracks, and when I was stationed there it contained two raccoons, an ocelot, a boa constrictor, two spider monkeys, a paranoid coati, a three-toed sloth, and a toucan, which was the only bird. There were a few mule deer, but they were to big for the cages and wandered around the quadrangle. Usually a few white rats gamboled around the sleepy boa's cage, showing him no respect until they became lumps in his body.

The sloth just hung on the same bit of fencing until the Corporal in command of the zoo thought he would die in captivity and released him. It took a full month for the strange creature to cross the quadrangle and disappear into the trees.

The Corporal mounted a monkey on a deer's back to take their picture together, but the mean little monkey turned around and took a bite-sized piece out of the deer's backside. My best friends were the toucan, the raccoons, and the deer. I sent home pictures of me comparing noses with the toucan, and a deer licking my face. This really made my mother nervous.

But the raccoons were my true pals. All day long the ocelot in the next cage would stalk them or stretch a paw into their cage which they would play with. Every morning I would put something edible in my breast pocket for them to eat, and they would reach in up to their armpits, dig it out and wash it in their drinking water before they ate it.

I used to enjoy going alone into the jungle and I was rewarded by some unique sights. Once I saw a group of unusually beautiful monkeys. They were mostly a very bright white, and were adorned with geometric black and sienna patches. They were playing follow-the-leader on a huge tree, swinging on a high branch, dropping about forty feet to a lower branch, and then climbing back up to repeat the performance. I looked them up in a book in the post library, and found out that they are not represented in any zoo or found anywhere else but in Panama, and that they cannot be kept alive in captivity.

One day I saw a red road coming out of the jungle, but when I came close to it I was shocked to see that it was a nation of soldier ants.

Oh yes, and one night when I was walking home to our apartment in Detroit, I was about to pass a woman when she began to sob. She was standing in the bright light that came from a butcher shop, and she had a raccoon on a leash. I asked if I could help her, and she tearfully pointed into the window there two flayed raccoons hung on hooks. "How could they do that to such sweet, lovable, little animals?" I knew why but she really didn't want an answer.

Things are much less exotic these days. I have been feeding some birds from a squirrel-proof feeder. When we moved into our house, the space between the roof and inner ceiling was occupied by a starling family. Once I mounted a twenty-foot ladder to return a baby starling to its nest, but its daddy showed no gratitude, and continued to dive at us whenever we left the house. One day a squirrel got interested in the starling's quarters and began to enlarge the opening to it. So I had to cover the opening with a piece of tin.

The neighborhood children noticed my interest in wildlife, and one morning six of them rang my door bell and told me that a bunch of baby robins had fallen out of their nest and were hopping all over my front lawn. Their nest was still in my maple tree and I shooed all of the babies into a cardboard carton, got a ladder, and then coaxed them back into the nest. About ten minutes later I looked out and saw that they were all back on the lawn, but this time they were accompanied by their momma. As I watched, she lined them up across my fence and showed them how to fly across the street one by one. I had only been a pain in the neck.

Then there was the wonderful field mouse who had hidden her eight tiny babies neatly lined up on a home made "mattress"" in the drawer of a tiny dresser that my girls had used when they were little, and which I kept in the garage for odds and ends. I spread the "mattress" out on the floor with the tiny babies on it, unfolded two chairs and waited with my son to see what would happen. The brave little momma peeked out furtively from behind a pile of logs we kept for firewood, then dashed out eight times to lift up a baby in her mouth and race back to the woodpile to hide it.

Currently I am feeding the fourth or fifth generation of a squirrel family which one by one have learned to climb out on my kitchen window where I leave four peanuts. The latest one is quite small and less alert and occasionally blue jays will beat him to my peanuts. Squirrels have a hard life, it seems. I have seen them chased by my nest door neighbors' cats, and one day by a hawk.

But they are pretty smart, and one day I accidentally brought out five peanuts instead of the usual four and they left one. I told Steffany Herzig, then eight years old about it, and she scoffed. "What's so great about that? I can count to a hundred."

I also told the story to my grandson Evan, who was about five and a half, when my son, Matthew called me from Fairbanks, Alaska, where he was teaching sculpture at the University. Evan said, "I can count to seven!"

Chapter XII
GAMES THAT PEOPLE PLAY

In my time I have written, not one, but many festoes, trying to map my way through an infinite number of roads that my creative impulses have opened. As most credible map-makers do, I only map territories already covered by my stumbling feet, perhaps to make certain not to stumble along the same path again. Probably my best manifesto was, "Never be dumb enough to paint yourself into a corner."

In my latest (or should I say, my last) one-man show, at the Jewish Community Center, north of the Vestal Plaza and east of Binghamton University, "Games That People Play and Other Important Matters," I found that my most recent art works, a series of Neo-Dada board games, had stumbled upon a fundamental aspect of humanity that links us to all forms of life in this universe. Just as any other animal, we are continually striving to create and hang on to our own spaces.

Just as it is true that humor isn't always something to laugh at, games are more than activities to pass time. Occasionally, they barely mask a competitiveness as brutal as life; they can cause permanent rifts, or sometimes build bridges between people. All of the factors in any human relationship can be present in games.

My great-uncle Harry, for example, was generous enough to let me beat him at chess when I was a teenager, to provide an excuse to give me five dollars as a prize from time to time. When I told this to my uncle Joe, the doctor, all he said was that Harry wasn't much of a chess player anyway.

Joe used to play chess with me often while reading *The Sunday New York Times* in the next room, telling me his moves though the standard numbering system. One day after about twenty moves I yelled, "Checkmate!" He came running into the room accusing me of erroneously moving one of his pieces. He went over the entire game in his head. He had that sort of memory. He could not find an "error," but he never played me again.

Something similar happened when I was about fifteen. I went for a ride with him, and he stopped at a driving range. He drove off a bucket of golf balls, stopping at the last one and saying, "Gee, I should have let you try it." He set the last one on the tee, and showed me how to hold the club and swing. My drive toppled the *275-yard* distance marker, about *25* yards beyond his best shot. He frowned and said, "Well, you're taller than me," and that was the end of my golf career.

When I was about twenty, I worked as a shipping clerk in Mangel's Stores' New York City warehouse. I used to play chess during the lunch hour, mostly with Willy Schultz, a German refugee about my age who memorized famous games. I beat him every time we played. He kept saying that I was making the "wrong" moves, which meant that I was doing something unlike what had been done in the game he had memorized. My reply was, "That's why the Americans always beat the Krauts."

When I was in the Service at First Army Headquarters, I used to play chess with an amazing old man. He was Heinrich Luks, the kid brother of George Luks, a genre painter who had been part of the "Ashcan School," a group of artists who flourished prior to the First World War. Heinrich had been an outstanding chess tournament player. In his prime, he had rarely lost a match. He had become unusually adept at playing for draws and stalemates in order to stave off defeats.

When we played, he was absolutely silent when it was his move, but when it was my turn he would try to distract me by singing old German songs and talking to himself in German, just loud enough to be heard.

He started out by beating me ten times. Then we played ten draws and stalemates. He would lay his traps as far as eight moves ahead. But then, I finally won a game, and another, and another, until our score was ten for him, ten ties, and ten for me; and he would in no way play another game and give me chance to forge ahead.

Later on, during the War, I dropped into a U.S.O. in New Orleans; the General Beauregard U.S.O. where a woman told me that if Beauregard had not been outnumbered, "He would have whipped the damned Yankees!"

As I walked past a table in the U.S.O. upon which a chess set was arranged for a game, a Corporal who was seated there asked me if I would like to play. His accent reminded me of Felix and Johnny Mujica, two Puerto Rican brothers who had been in my Simpson Street gang. I sat down and he held out his hands hiding two pieces for me to chose one, and I selected the one with a white piece and had first move.

After my second move, he said, "You are trying to beat me with a fool's mate." "No," I said, "The thought never entered my mind."

At the third move, he said, "Yes, yes, you think I am a fool. That is why you are trying for a fool's mate."

I sensed trouble. "Look," I said, "If you know what a fool's mate is, why are you making the moves that open you up to it?"

I moved for the fourth time, and before he made his answering move he said, "Definitely, you think I am a fool, so you are trying for a fool's mate."

I moved my fifth piece and said, "Checkmate," and I got up and left him, cursing under his breath. If a man is a fool, what can you do?

After the war, when I was teaching at the City College of New York, my old alma mater, I used to play Professor Stanley Meltzoff, who was the most talented player I ever faced. He was a Blitzkrieg player, who seemed to place you under instant attack in three or four moves. One day I told him about Heinrich Luks, saying that once I beat someone, they never can win against me again.

He snorted, but after trimming me eight times, he overreached himself, and I won. From then on, I won again and again, and he would say things like, "It just is not possible! It can't be like that! You have hypnotized me! It's a hex! I can't believe it."

And there was my good friend, Morty Fried, an Anthropologist, in fact chairmen of his Department at Columbia, who had also been a mentor to my cousin, Michael Moerman. Morty and I had played one another quite a few times, and he had never won. I began to understand why one day. He and his wife, Martha, were all packed to leave for China for his field work, and we were playing a game while I flipped through the *Sunday Times*. Suddenly I noticed how quiet he was, and I felt a palpable tension in the air. I checked out the game, and to my astonishment I noticed that he had three attacks poised to give him his first victory, but that he had used none of them. I launched an attack with my knights, broke up his formations, and won. Over the years he had become so conditioned to losing, that even with a triply-guaranteed victory, he had lacked the confidence to pull the trigger.

Who says that games are only pastimes?

Oh yeah. A few years ago I took a snapshot of Alison and Steve, my grandchildren, playing chess as a team against me. Of course, I won.

About a month before I was thirteen, my mom said, "We have to do something about his Bar Mitzvah. His grandfolks would enjoy it." She took me to the nearest synagogue, where the Rabbi said that I might just be able to learn the Hebrew alphabet enough to read from the Torah, and maybe I could memorize a speech.

The Rabbi introduced me to his assistant, a young redheaded

Rabbinical Student who would be my teacher. The Assistant said in Yiddish, "This is a big one. I bet he knows how to box." He held up his dukes and I promptly punched him under the eye, knocking off his hat. "He can," " he said, "He can."

Morale: Don't challenge street kids.

The summer my dad died, my mother went for an operation, and I went to stay with my grandparents for three weeks.

The first day that I went down into the street, I walked past a bunch of guys who were standing around and talking. They greeted me and we introduced ourselves. The biggest guy, a redhead who was an inch or two taller than me, whispered to his kid brother who ran into their house and came out with two pairs of boxing gloves.

"How's about sparring with me?" Red asked. I nodded, thinking that he must be pretty good if he owned two pairs of gloves. He was jabbing at me from all angles. I cocked my right first and threw my first punch. He blocked it easily, but kept backing away, almost going through someone's basement window to get away. "Time," he yelled, and I stopped going after him. He shook his right arm and rubbed it. He had taken my punch on his biceps, and he said that he could not keep his right arm up to block my punches.

Anyway, I ruined Red's summer, catching every ball he hit and hitting line drives over his head. One of the guys gave me the nickname, "Waco." I guess he didn't dare call me "Wacko."

Later that summer, a neighbor who was a middleweight boxer on the City College team, asked me to spar with him, "because I was just about the right size."

He was jabbing me all over at will until I realized that he was a left-hander, so I switched around to mirror his stance and hit him with a right 'jab' to his jaw. He held on and said, "O.K., that's enough." He told me that he was not used to dealing with "right-handed lefties."

I once participated in what must have been the shortest stick-ball game in history. It took us over an hour to chose up sides and then swap players to even things out. I was the first batter and I hit the first ball bounced to me way up on a line. The ball went into the upper opening of a window that was open top and bottom, rolled down the window shade and came out through the opening at the bottom only to be caught by one of their outfielders. I watched in amusement as the window-shade rolled up with a loud snap and a woman ran over in shock.

Both teams argued to no avail for about another hour before we decided to quit. We could not decide to accept it either as a home-run or an out without having made prior ground-rules to anticipate such a freak occurrence.

Once, in a sandlot softball game I hit a grounder to third base. As I arrived at first, the first baseman, stretching for a wild throw, hit my eyeglasses and broke the right lens, filling my eyelid with glass splinters. My friends took me to my uncle Joe's office around the corner.

I was too groggy to make it alone.

Uncle Joe took out all of the glass, but he wanted me to see his friend Dr. Fried, an eye surgeon and author of a book on his specialty. Dr. Fried examined me and told me that my right eye was useless, that it was a birth defect, "a lazy eye;" and that since my other eye was so nearsighted, he advised me not to go into any profession that would require me to rely upon my vision. This was a total surprise to me. I had never noticed it; I had close to a 500 on base percentage in my sandlot games.

The funny thing was that the doctors who gave me my Army Physical about eight years later, were not put off by my "lazy eye", but then, they took in 48,000 men in December of 1943, the month that I was drafted. The "lazy eye" made it a little difficult to fire a rifle with much accuracy. They were designed for right-eyed soldiers, and in order to get my left eye to the gun sights and line them up with the target, I had to twist my neck across the rifle stock. After an hour on the range, my right cheekbone made me look as if I had lost a fight.

One day on the range at Fort Niagara, during a basic Refresher course (luckily I had not had a first basic), after a slew of "Maggie's Drawers," a red flag that meant I had missed the entire target, I began to collect one bull's eye after another. As I shifted my position for greater comfort, I was surprised to see that I had gotten another bull's eye without even firing my rifle.

I looked to my right to see Sgt. Martin lifting his head from his rifle. I said, "Thanks Sarge." He grinned back, answering in his inimitable West Virginian drawl, "You couldn't hit a cow in the ass with a bull-fiddle."

In my recent one-man show I exhibited four board games, hence the title, "Games That People Play and Other Important Matters." At present I am creating my fifth board game: one of a set of neo-dada assemblages that appear to be illegitimate offspring of chess sets. The pieces are assembled from tool handles, drawer knobs, staircase newels, balustrade spindles, etc., painted in bright enamels and fastened permanently to playing boards lined with grids of exotic woods.

The first game is *"Inertia,* the Perfect Board Game." The rules tell us that "There are no age limits. It can be played by pre-natal individuals of any sexual persuasion, or by those who are a thousand or more years old. It may be played by as few as no players up to an infinite number of players, or even players in leagues of various sorts. The game has no rules, and there are no possible moves. As a result, there are no strategies and no developments possible. And best of all, there are no winners or losers."

The second game is game is called *"Consensus,* a New, Exciting Board Game by the Creator of *Inertia."*

Consensus may be enjoyed by players of any age or whatever sex. It can be used as a form of solitaire if it pleases you, or indulged in by any number of players who must all be on the same side.

In practice, the sixteen players on the Red, White, and Blue Team take turns stomping the lone player on the other "team" into a hole in the board. "The game continues until you are called in to dinner."

"Fair Game, an enjoyable new game, is brought to you by the creator of *Inertia* and *Consensus,* both of which are already sweeping the country. In *Fair Game* there are two teams, the Big Team and the Little Team. Members of the Big Team may move any number of squares in any direction until they land on a square occupied by a member of the Little Team.

"The Big Team then takes over the square in which he has landed, and the Little Team member is removed from the board and dropped into one of the black boxes provided on each side of the board. The Little Team has no moves at all. When the entire Little Team has been removed from the board, the Big Team is declared to be the winner. As you can see, there is a distinct advantage to being on the Big Team."

The game *Process* was inspired by my last conversation with Professor Bob Pennfield, who knew that he did not have long to live. He was understandably a little depressed, and when I pointed out that "We are all dealt different hands in life, but it doesn't matter, because in the end, the House always wins," the thought seemed to cheer him up.

Anyway, "In this new exciting game of skill and chance, there is a large black ball suspended from a hand crank. The ball is set in motion by turning the crank handle. As the pieces on the board are knocked over, they are removed and placed into the little black boxes that are provided. The rules are the same as in gambling establishments or in life, itself, The House Always Wins."

Game number five, which I am currently assembling, is called *Uneasy Truce*. It is "an excellent board game" but not for a fine sunny day when you had rather be doing something more active outside. The two teams are separated only by a narrow red boarder, waiting to be activated. Everything is in a potential state, brimming with explosive power, requiring only human intervention to produce havoc and destruction.

There are no rules or other restraints. The game liberates the destructive imagination, allowing a player to visualize the ultimate and complete obliteration of the opponent's forces; but this urge is tempered by the suspicion that one's opponent has an equally aggressive intention plus, possibly, some unforseen and unexpected, but nevertheless, unbeatable advantage. Since, in the same way, your opponent is equally uncertain about your hidden assets, trepidation and hesitancy on both sides helps to maintain a condition of uneasy waiting

Come to think of it; did you ever wonder who invented chess? No one really knows, but I would bet that it was a woman. The queen, after all, is the most powerful piece. She can rocket around the board like a loose cannon. The king is a handicap. He has to be protected by the entire army of pieces. He is feeble, limping one box at a time. If you did not have to continually protect him, you would probably never lose. Your opponent would have to take every one of your pieces off the board in order to beat you.

Or could the inventor have been gay?

I hope that you have read and enjoyed everything up to this point. If not, at least try to see the movie.

Chapter XIII
THE LIVES AND TIMES OF RAOUL SCHLEPPMANN

Dedicated to Richard F. Shepard and Morton H. Fried

The vital and intriguing artist Raoul Schleppmann was discovered during an otherwise uneventful day during World War II by three old friends and fellow scholars, graduates of the City College of New York, who, by chance, one evening, found themselves momentarily united on the streets of New York City. They were on their way to hot pastrami sandwiches and celery tonic at Katz's Delicatessen, when they began to discuss the predictable phoniness of official biographies of famous people. To counter this dismaying tendency, they "discovered" the remarkable mid-European artist, Raoul Schleppmann, already coming up with many ideas for future research.

The three friends were then PFC Morton Fried, who was one day to chair the Department of Anthropology at Columbia University, Richard F. Shepard, radio operator on the astonishingly decrepit merchant ship, the Mauna Kea (which kept goats on its poop deck), who was later to become a highly respected reporter at The New York Times, and the then Corporal Irving Zupnick (yours truly), who, after a checkered academic career, was to retire as a professor in the Department of Art and Art History at Binghamton University in Vestal, New York.

They continued to "research" Raoul over the hot pastrami and celery tonic, but a few days later, they dispersed to return to their vital roles in the War.

This placed the burden of writing the first draft of "The Lives and Times of Raoul Schleppmann" in the capable hands of Dick, who was Radio Operator on the Mauna Kea, a ship with the crucial mission of worldwide distribution of Pepto-Bismol, the then secret weapon against Army Chow. Dick wrote the original draft on the backs of radio message forms during the many hours in which he was forbidden to use his radio, lest it attract German U-Boats eager to cut off the supply of vital Pepto-Bismol and thus shorten the War.

During this pregnant moment, Mort Fried wrote to Irv Zupnick about his awful tour of duty as a Combat Engineer in Columbus, Georgia, which is as far as one can get from human civilization, and where, in spite of his asthma, he was forced to wear his gas mask all day long, probably to make sure he would not misplace it. It just so happened that Zupnick, being in First Army headquarters, had heard that the Army was going to set up a Chinese language program at Harvard University. He urged Mort to apply for it, and Mort was accepted, preparing the way for him to become the leading authority on Chinese social structure after the War.

The O.S.S. was preparing those in the Chinese program to be parachuted into the southern, Cantonese provinces, but typically, the Army had been teaching the soldiers Mandarin, or northern Chinese, which, they eventually discovered would be unintelligible to the Cantonese. It would have been almost as futile as speaking English in remote areas of Alabama and Mississippi.

The Harvard Chinese program was broken up, and Mort Fried, with his Chinese background, according to Army Logic, was assigned to the Cooks' and Bakers' School in Camp Crowder, Missouri. It is conceivable, on the basis of Army Logic, that the O.S.S. then planned to open a chain of restaurants across China as a network for information and chronic diarrhea.

Irv Zupnick, now a Sergeant, outranking his dad, bounced around various Army posts, ending in Panama, where he spent his final year of military service, trying to disrupt military discipline as best he could. During his tour of duty there, Dick Shepard called him as the Mauna Kea slinked through the Canal on its clandestine unheralded mission, but the two friends were unable to meet or even wave to one another. The Canal Authority was in some haste to get the Mauna Kea through the Canal, fearing that it would sink, and that its unauthorized goats would escape into the jungle.

When World War II no longer required their awesome support, the three friends were reunited in New York City, where they worked at creating their careers in the 'Real World'.

By that time, Mort was in the Anthropology Department at Columbia University, Dick was doing weather and shipping news reports at The New York Times, and Irv was a Teaching Fellow at C.C.N.Y.

While still a Teaching Fellow at City College, Irv and his friend Sam Salant, who was President of the student's Art History Club, came up with the idea of introducing these future art historians, and the Art Department faculty, to the remarkable Raoul Schleppmann, by inviting the distinguished Art Historian, Richard F. Shepard, to lecture on the up-to-then little-known artist.

To make the proper entrance, Dick borrowed Mort Fried's briefcase, which was stuffed with his Doctoral Dissertation.

Before Dick entered, Sam Salant did a nasty thing, explaining to the assembled group that Professor Shepard was a bit eccentric, but also very sensitive, and that if they noticed anything strange, they should try not to laugh.

Then in came Dick, a Daily Worker sticking out of his left pocket, and a Christian Science Monitor out of the right. On his lapel, he wore a pin of World War I vintage that proclaimed, "Gott Strafe England!"

Dick placed Mort's briefcase on the desk and began to spread its contents, the unbound manuscript of Fried's dissertation (to Mort's horror) all over the desk. Then he took out an ashtray, complete with a lit cigar, which he began to puff at vigorously. Dick had a puzzled look on his face, because none of the audience was laughing at his antics, and Mort, Sam and Irv were on the floor, out of sight, trying to keep their laughter from being noticed.

Dick began reading with the information that Raoul was born in the tiny Balkan town of Naharodny-Naharoshoe, which caused a war between Serbia and Croatia, because neither country wanted such an insignificant town that took up so much map space. Eventually the problem was solved by reducing the town to a garbage dump, but the enmity over this border-dispute-in-reverse continues until this day.

Raoul was the first artist to emerge from the Schleppmann family, all of whom had worked at the local Wendy's. His kid brother, Ernesto, who spelled the family name "Schlepppmann," in order not to be confused with his brother (which made it difficult to pronounce), became a sculptor. Ernesto, unfortunately, could only work in soft materials such as snow, butter, or Cream of Wheat, after permanently injuring both wrists while slam-dunking doughnuts into coffee cups (but more about him later).

Raoul was extremely short in stature, never growing to be more than four feet tall, which was a distinct disadvantage in those days, when the best paying artistic commissions consisted of grandiose historical murals. Because of his limited reach and the absence of ladders in those days, he had to work with taller artists, and limited himself to the lower half of murals. For this reason, he soon acquired the sobriquet, "Master of the Belt Buckle."

A rare, possibly the only example of his skill in designing belt buckles, is to be seen in the small panel, "The Rape of Europa." Raoul, with his innate honesty, which contributed to his isolation, portrayed the true story, not the false one invented by the courtiers of her father's court, showing the avid Princess in the act of raping the bull, and not the other way around, as it is usually portrayed.

Raoul began his career as an apprentice to Duddy Kravitz, formerly his kindergarten teacher, who moonlighted by painting "Herren" or "Frauen" on doors in Naharodny- Naharoshoe. The young Raoul found this to be so boring that he almost gave up his artistic career until he switched his apprenticeship to Storto Pescefacci, a lost Venetian, who often sketched models in the nude (the models being in the nude), and this revived the young man's interest.

It was just at this inauspicious moment in Raoul's career that he was to embark on a project that was to have far-reaching consequences for the history of art. This discovery was made by Irv Zupnick, Prof. Emeritus in Art History and former art columnist and reviewer whose work contributed to the demise of the Sun-Bulletin, which was absorbed by the Binghamton Press.

It all began when a German traveling salesman, Otto Von Kratzesel, amassed a collection of inexpensive artist's sketches while traveling in Venice and Padua, and then into the Lowlands, through Brussels and Amsterdam, before heading homewards. While on his way, an idea struck him: if he could find a cheap artist to translate these sketches into oil paintings, he could return to his native Frankfurt with startling evidence of his connoisseurship. He continued to travel, searching for a cheap painter, until he ran into Pescefacci, who sent him to Raoul.

At this point in his career, Schleppmann was an ideal choice for this job. He had studied with so many masters: Pescefacci, Duddy Kravitz, Presto Rubino, Miguel Manto, and Dom DiMaggio, that he had no style of his own, and could easily paint in whatever style was suggested by the many sketches.

Kratzesel returned to Frankfurt with these paintings and married a friend's granddaughter, only to die a week later of a massive coronary. The young widow, cleaning up after the funeral, sold several hundred paintings to a traveling junk-dealer, who then resold them on his travels through Europe.

As a result, there are hundreds of paintings attributed to unknown masters: "School of Fontainbleu, ca. 1430," "Early Sixteenth Century Viennese," "Dutch Master of the Half-Length," "Late Sixteenth Century Flemish," or "Venetian, ca. 1520s," to name a few.

Zupnick's discovery, that they were all the work of Raoul Schleppmann, has sent museum and gallery curators all over the world (including Texas), in an effort to relabel those works; and it is rumored that a massive exhibition of these paintings by Raoul will be assembled at Nice or Omsk or Leesville, Louisiana. As Dr. Zupnick has demonstrated through an agonizingly stylistic analysis, Raoul's style of this period, such as it is, is easily identified by its lack of skill, strange distortions, and poor sense of color.

During this period of Raoul's frantic activity, his younger brother, Ernesto Schlepppmannn, was hired by King Victor the Vacillator, of Upper Badoo, who has been credited with "The Forty Years of Peace," since he was unable to decide which country to attack or when. He hired Ernesto to do an equestrian portrait, probably either in snow, smooth peanut butter, or Cream of Wheat. Poor Ernesto waited around for months as King Victor the Vacillator kept growing and shaving his beard and mustache and changing his wigs. There was also the problem of the horse, an important prop in an equestrian portrait. King Victor the Vacillator, who actually hated horses, could not decide whether he should attempt to ride the animal, stand beside it, or leave himself out of the composition.

It is noted in the King's memoirs, so full of erasures and crossings-out, that the artist "jumped into the moat," either out of "frustration," or "the fenestration," where his body created much merriment, either among "the dragons" or "the dragoons."

Finally, it is worth mentioning that according to a letter reportedly written by Igor Rizzuto to Count Marcel Plotz, Raoul discovered one morning, the perspective vanishing point two days and forty-five minutes before the Florentine, Brunelleschi. He then went out to have a pizza with pepperoni and a celery tonic, and when he returned he looked for the vanishing point, but somehow, it had disappeared.

In any case, I, Irving L. Zupnick, have enjoyed studying that fascinating artist, Raoul Schleppmann. He was a regular feature of my April First Lectures, a memento of which, I received from my Graduate Students at the Fifth Schleppmann Symposium in 1970.

I now realize that my friends were the brothers I missed out on, and women the sisters I would have cherished-- except for one who is still and will forever be in my heart.

Let's close with one of Dick Shepard's favorite songs, 'The Erie Bargeman's Shanty:'

The Er-i-ee was a risin' and the gin a-gettin'
low,
And we'd scarcely think we'd get a drink
Till we'd get to Buffalo-o-o
Till we'd get to Buffalo.

Oh, the Captain, he got married,
And the Cook he went to jail,
So, I guess that I'm the only son-of-a-gun
Who's left to tell the tale-o
Who's left to tell the tale.

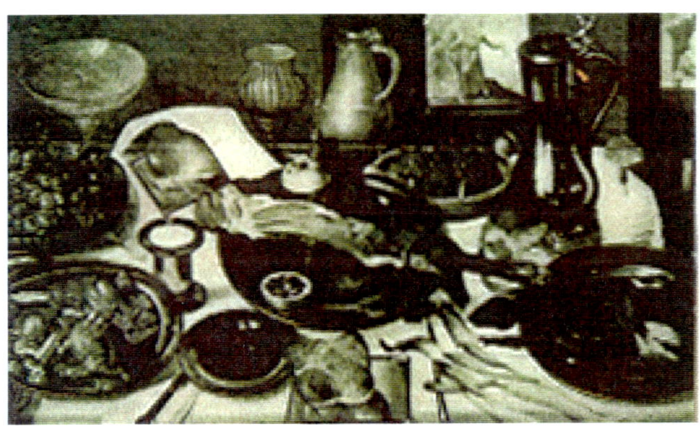

Figure 1: Raoul Schleppmann. (Formerly, ca. 1580 Flemish.) BEFORE THE LAST SUPPER. Eindhoven, The Abbe Museum.

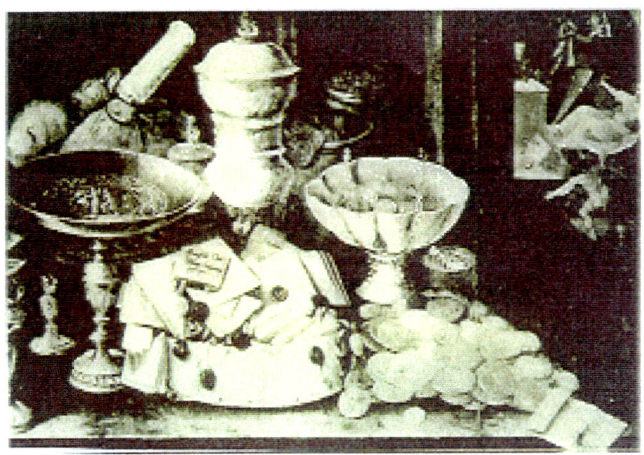

Figure 2: Raoul Schleppmann. (Formerly, Sixteenth Century Flemish, School of Francken.) THE LAST DAYS OF JUDAS. Sold in the Vienna Art Market in 1920.

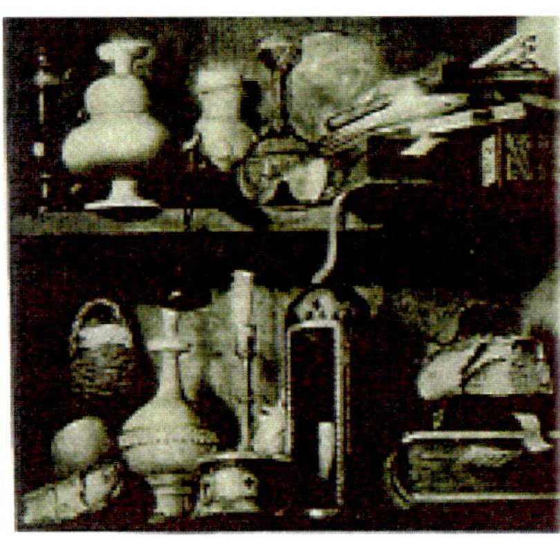

Figure 3: Raoul Schleppmann. (Formerly Flemish Master of 1538.) WHAT LOT LEFT. Oterle, Rijksmuseum

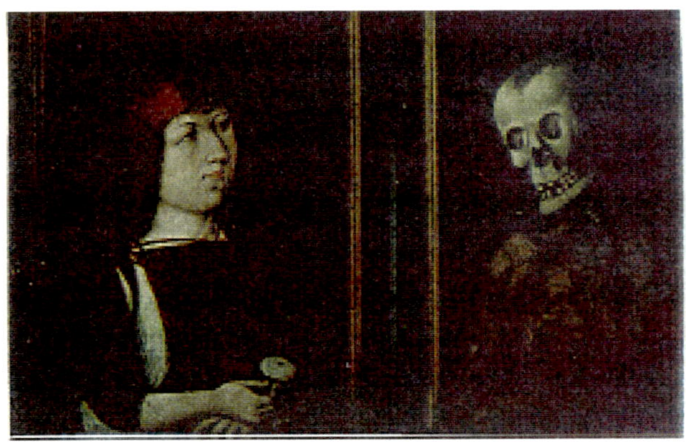

Figure 4: Raoul Schleppmann. (Formerly, Basel Master of 1487.) HIERONYMOUS TSCHKKENBURLIN AND HIS FIRST WIFE. Basel, Kunsmuseum.

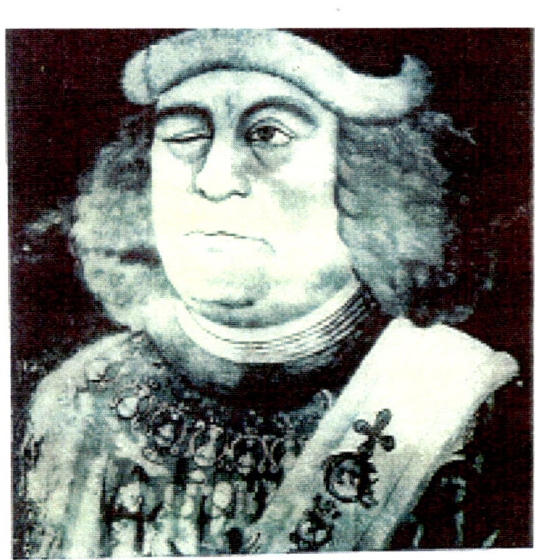

Figure 5: Raoul Schleppmann. (Formerly 1432 S. Tyrol School.) OSWALD VON WOLKENSTEIN. The Wolkenstein Collection, Key West, Florida.

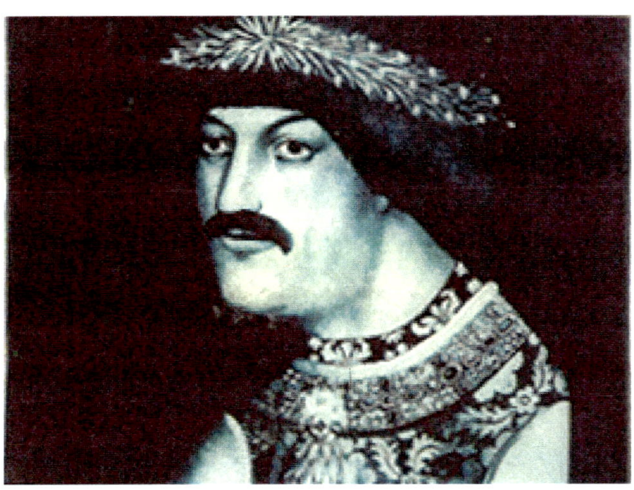

Figure 6: Raoul Schleppmann. (Formerly Fifteen Century Auatrian, circa 1435.) DUKE ALBERT V. Vienna, Kunsthistorische Museum

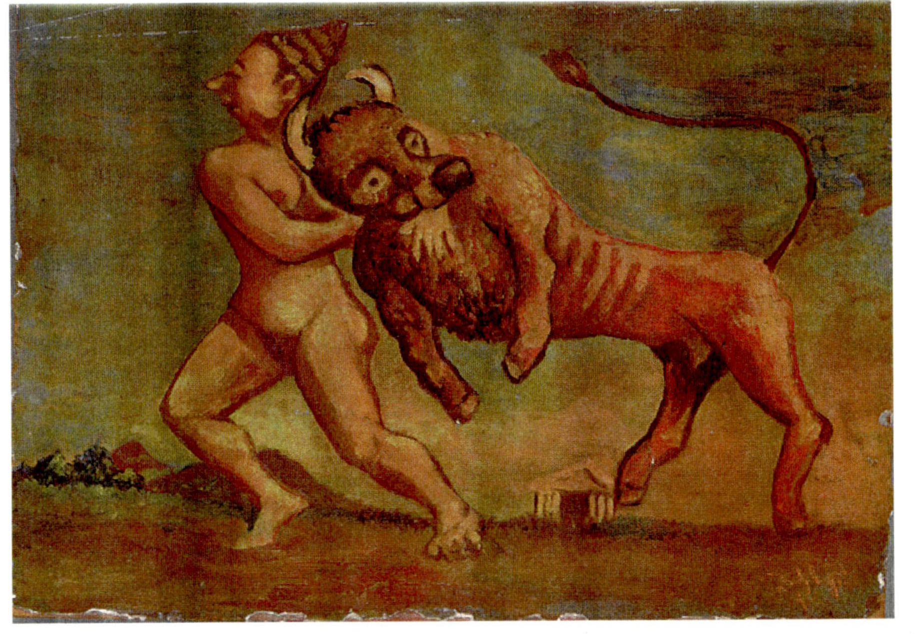

Figure 7: Raoul Schleppmann. Study for a belt buckle. THE RAPE OF EUROPE. Private Collection. Vestal, New York.

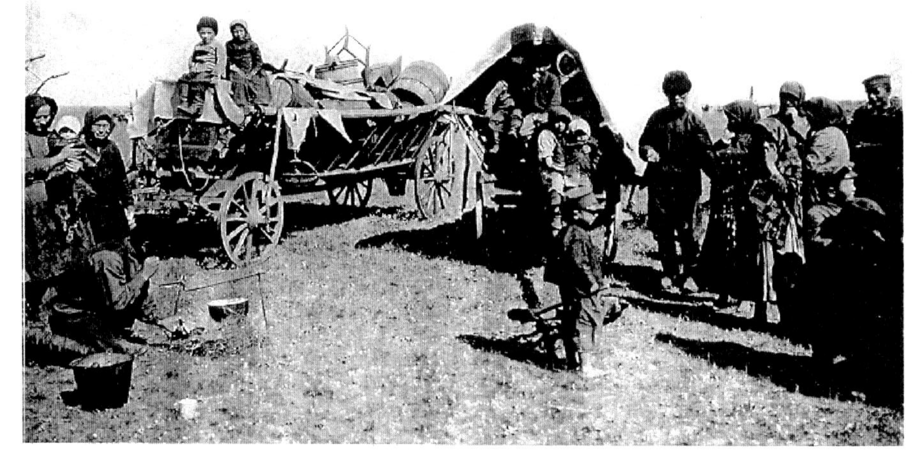

Figure 8: The Fifth Annual Schleppmann Festival (1970). Members of the Art Department Cluster around State vehicles before lunch. (SUNY BInghamton).